Testimonials

By Anne Stone

At first I was a bit intimidated by the title; however, after reading the introduction, I knew this was a book I wanted to read. Mary's writing style is very "user friendly," and she has a great message. I enjoyed the book so much and shared various sections with a friend who also ended up buying the book and loving it!!! I didn't really understand feng shui very well before reading this book, but I did realize that my environment plays a big part in how I feel and what happens in my life. Mary has studied and thoroughly understands many disciplines and how they affect our well-being and is able to weave them together to help you to make your environment supportive to your body, mind, and spirit. I am not a writer and cannot do this book justice . . . if you read it, you will be glad that you did.

By Brooklyn Morris

This book incorporates the metaphysical and spiritual aspects of feng shui in an exciting and inspiring way. I loved the writing style; unlike most feng shui books, this one is very easy to follow and goes deeper into the metaphysical and meditation.

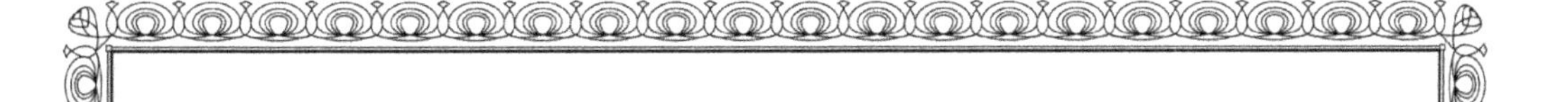

The Alchemy *of* Quantum Mind Feng Shui

Science within Spirituality

Spirituality within Science

Guide to Understanding Your Potential

Updated and Expanded Edition

The Alchemy *of* Quantum Mind Feng Shui

Mary Shurtleff
CHT, FSID

The Alchemy of Quantum Mind Feng Shui

Cover and interior design by Ted Ruybal.

ISBN 13: 978-0-9830892-1-6

ISBN 10: 0-9830892-1-3

LCCN: 2010940770

Second Edition

2 3 4 5 6 7 8 9 10

This is a Wisdom House product, published by Wisdom House Books.

www.wisdomhousebooks.com

For information, please contact:

Mary Shurtleff

Design Wisdom-Feng Shui

801-573-4042

www.maryshurtleff.com

Shurtleff, Mary L., 1953–

Reconnecting Your Spirit: 2008

The Alchemy of Quantum Mind Feng Shui: 2006

A Reference Guide for Students of Feng Shui: 1997

Note: This author has extensively researched all sources within her grasp to ensure the accuracy of the information contained in this book. Working with energy contains such a broad base of information and intuition that it is impossible for each practitioner or nonprofessional to agree with all information given. Some data in this book are the findings of the actual observations by this author of her clients.

We assume no responsibility for errors, inaccuracies, omissions, or any inconsistency within. No slight is intended to individuals or organizations.

Mary is an interior designer feng shui practitioner, certified hypnotherapist, and a theta healer/intuitive anatomy/ six-sensory practitioner; she has based her information and opinions upon her and her clients' life experiences, and she has gathered reliable information from others in the energy field and the field of the healing arts. Mary is not a doctor and is not connected to the medical field in any way. This book is not to be used as a substitute for medical care. Always consult your health care provider for any questions you may have about your physical health.

Dedication

I dedicate this book to all the people who have helped me become the person I am today. Those people include my family, friends, clients, and teachers. You have each touched my life in such a unique way. I would especially like to thank Virgil Hayes and Betty Finnas, two clinical hypnotherapist instructors in the Salt Lake City Valley who believed in me. Without Betty and Virgil, I would not have the self-confidence and courage to pursue my dreams and be doing what I love to do today, which is helping people improve their lives.

I would also like to thank Lillian Garnier Bridges for introducing me to the word *feng shui* in 1992 at a seminar in Salt Lake City, Utah. I thought the term feng shui sounded so "out there." But little did I know that she was opening a door to me to begin searching and learning about that funny term, feng shui. Today I am happily making a living doing feng shui interior design. I now know Lillian knew what she was talking about, and I do not miss a chance to hear her speak when we are in the same area. Thank you, Lillian.

I would also like to thank my other primary mentors of feng shui. They include my Sifu, Peter Leung of Toronto, Canada, Grandmaster Professor Lin Yun, and Helen and James Jay. Thank you also, Tao Tan, an acupuncturist in Salt Lake City, Utah, for helping me understand how Chinese medicine, acupressure, and Chinese philosophy all fit into feng shui.

I would also like to acknowledge Louise Hay, Florence Scovel Shinn, and Sonia Choquette for their inspiring contributions to the service of man. I encourage everyone to pick up one of their books. They unknowingly have inspired me to find my true potential.

I would like to say thank you to my mother and father for giving me a safe and good home and foundation to start my journey through life and to my siblings for teaching me the ropes about how life works outside of our safe home.

Last, but not least, I would like to thank my husband Brad and daughters Angelique and Jessica for being my guinea pigs during my studies. Thank you also to my step-in children, Carly, Paul, and Mandi. Thank you for being a part of my life.

Thank you also to my extended family and friends, who have made important contributions to my life. I would also like to thank my clients, who have allowed me to learn from them as much as they have learned from me. Without that experience, I could not be doing what I am doing today.

I love you all.

Table of Contents

A Message of Hope From Mary

Greetings! Since you have picked this book up, there is already an energy connection between you and me. This book was originally written to help you discover how to adjust your thinking and your environment to help you to manifest your dreams into a reality. This edition has been updated, expanded, and revised to better explain how to help you examine and analyze the aspects in your life to improve prosperity, health, and relationships. I have learned to do this, and so can you.

Through the years, I have learned to see beyond what is physically there and to trust metaphysically what is really there, unseen, lurking in the silence of myself and others. I started to dissect my life by following the trail of familial programming that I learned from the womb to the present day. This journey helped me understand why I had shaped and molded my life the way I did. I then had to cut the cord to my old tales of woe, despair, victimization, and martyrdom. I was amazed at who I found. Me.

I now live a magical life. I always did; I just did not understand the hidden meanings and metaphors within it that guided me. I made my life harder than it needed to be. Once we are able to understand the meanings behind our lives, they can be joyous adventures. There are happy endings.

If you dedicate and apply yourself, this book can teach you how to move through your life more peacefully and prosperously, helping you discover and live your life's purpose. Quantum Mind Feng Shui shows you how to clear the old collective debris from your thoughts, your emotions, your body, and your home and how to replace them with new, productive goals.

"Whatever you judge, condemn, and resist in the inner world persists both internally and externally."

—Niroshanna Mandalanayagam

You must set up your physical environment to match your newfound emotional changes and thoughts. Everything holds a level of vibration or energy. Feng shui simply means the movement of energy and the effect it has upon your body. When you change the vibration of your behavior, the vibration or message of your environment must change as well. Feng shui is far more than furniture placement or worrying about where to put your bed. Feng shui reflects patterns of behavior resulting in the way you design your home. Change is assured when these patterns of behavior and the vibration levels of your home are altered, updated, or eliminated.

To learn and execute Quantum Mind Feng Shui effectively, it is important for you to connect with your higher self or a higher power outside yourself. This message is not about religion or a judgmental right or wrong; it is simply about finding your inner voice and desires and discovering what is right for you.

We are all spiritual because we all have a spirit or essence that guides us. Where does this spirit come from? Where do those inspirations within your soul come from? They have to come from somewhere.

Unfortunately, because of our need to be politically correct, it has become politically incorrect to call this spirit or higher power God. However, for all intents and purposes, that is what it is. The word *God* means a higher power from which we seek wisdom. However, find the word that makes you feel most comfortable. Some call it nature, universe, cosmos, Great Spirit, Buddha, Jesus, etc.—choose whatever makes sense to you. You may call it Yoda if that makes you more comfortable; I do not care. The most important thing of all is that you access the thought continuum to your spirit to gain wisdom and insight to manifest your thoughts and dreams into materialized reality.

I would like to share some of the weaknesses, fears, and successes of my life. In part, these experiences brought this book to life today. I want you to feel that you know me.

Even though I speak of family turmoil and crisis, I want everyone to understand that my childhood was good. Some things just went bad and out of anyone's control. My mother was a good mom and my father a hardworking man who supported his family. As in any family, there is a pecking order or family position. Generally speaking, the birth position of siblings may affect the way a child reacts to various situations in his or her life path. With each position in the family, there are expectations or lack of expectations that affect a child's life path.

If you interviewed three children in the same family, you would never know the same parents raised those children because each experience is different. No one can stop your experience. No amount of good or bad parenting can stop the motion of your life path and your personal reaction to it. Children do not come with a user's manual or worry-free guarantee.

As I speak of my experiences, they are in no way a bad reflection upon my father or mother. I am simply describing bad experiences in which they may or may not have been involved. I want to stress again that I love my mother and father and my siblings very deeply and would never do anything to intentionally hurt them; however, I do feel the need to share my story of how I found myself.

"I am what I am because of who we all are."

—Mother Teresa

This book was therapy for me and is part of my life's purpose to make a difference in the lives of others. I want to motivate. I want to inspire. Most importantly, I want you to understand your life and grow your dreams into your reality—just as I have been able to do.

I was raised in a small town in Wyoming. My father worked on the railroad as a track supervisor, and my mother was a stay-at-home mom. We were—by all financial standards—poor. The only indoor plumbing we had was a water faucet in the kitchen. We bathed in a metal tub and did our dishes in metal dishpans. Everything my dad earned was put toward living expenses and five growing children. There was no extra money for frivolous wants. My mom made all of my clothes by hand or they were hand-me-downs from my older sisters. My mother cut or permed my hair. It was short and simply styled.

My days were spent outdoors playing and imagining what life was like in the sky or in the other parts of the world. I loved books and loved seeing pictures of other places. I wanted to travel to those places. My mother once told me that if I dug a hole deep enough, I would reach China. I remember one day when I started digging and digging because I wanted to see what China was like.

Because there were five children in my family, the older ones paired up with each other, as did the younger two. I was usually too young for the older ones to play with and too old for the younger ones to be with, so I felt alone and lonely. During this time of loneliness, I learned that there were forces outside of myself with which to commune.

Some of my first childhood memories involve what society calls imaginary friends. Were they real or imagined? At the time, they seemed real, and they would tell me things about people and places that a child could not know.

We played mind games, and they showed me how to move my mind and watch from the side or above my physical body. When this happened, my body seemed numb and my mind felt unattached. I would observe with no emotion. In this altered state, I was able to do simple astro travel. I took my mind to places I had only seen in books, even China. For the most part, my life was full of wonderment, and I was happy.

I did not realize until I went to school how different the world was from the one in which I lived. School was my first exposure to people outside my circle of influence. I did not seem to fit in. A group of kids at school had apparently decided that I looked odd, and they would laugh at me, shove me, and call me names. The shoving actually hurt less than the teasing. They frequently called me "ugly" and teased me about being poor. I usually ended up crying, and the more I cried, the more they teased. I would end up in a "fight or flight" state.

The "fight or flight response" can be compared to a cornered cat. Cats are usually mellow until threatened. Once threatened, their claws and teeth come out, and they will fight just hard enough to run and get away from the situation, not caring how much damage they inflict along the way. Once away from the threatening situation, they revert to a state of quiet with a heightened awareness of their environment. The cat does not usually go around threatening people, but do not try to corner it! As a child, I quickly learned to show no emotion and to fight back to get away from any uncomfortable situation. Fighting back made me at least feel somewhat empowered.

School instilled in me a fear of others. I could not understand this new world. The kids there liked to hurt other people, and they laughed while they did it. I did not want to be around them, but something inside of me still wanted them to like me. I gained a heightened ability to "feel" my way around my environment. I learned to hang back, read people, and become invisible. I no longer trusted blindly. I learned to be the cornered cat.

I hated school. I was so confused. I had only one friend that first year of school, and she was as poor as I was. We would play and pretend that we were rich, wore beautiful clothes, and traveled the world.

Because of the outward stress, I found myself mind astro traveling at school constantly, causing me to be in trouble with the teachers for not paying attention. My perfect world of wonderment was shattered. I felt more lost and alone. Neither the teachers nor the kids seemed to like me. This caused me to travel more inside myself—into my world of imagination.

Even as a young child, I knew there was so much more to life than I was living and seeing. No matter what those teachers or kids did or said, I had a child's faith that my life was going to be wonderful. I would travel the world, meet famous people, and wear beautiful clothes—even if it were only in my mind.

At the age of six, I had an unexplainable experience, one in which I nearly drowned. I was staying with my father's sister for the summer. I was never away from home, and it was an adventure. My aunt decided to take me swimming, and she asked if I knew how. I had never been swimming before, but told her I could. How hard could it be, right?

When I got to the pool, I jumped into the deep end of the pool and sank immediately to the bottom. My body was somehow surrounded with an inverted pyramid of white light that lifted me from the water. I could see what was happening below. The white light was humming. It was strange, but enjoyable. I was, indeed, swimming.

The next thing I remember was lying on the side of the pool, coughing, with people staring at me. This experience was confusing, but it was one of peace and contentment, not fear. I thought it was swimming and I told everyone the same. My aunt, however, was not so happy with me.

A couple of years later, I jumped into the deep water again, and the strange experience recurred. I do not believe I had a near-death experience, but I definitely left my body and watched it from above. However, this time when I regained consciousness, I was frightened. The man who rescued me was yelling at me. I had told him I knew how to swim but then had floundered. Because of his fear, I am still very cautious of water. After this second incident, my mother put me in swimming lessons.

I believe that at this time in my childhood, the veil between Heaven and Earth was very thin for me. As a child, I experienced numerous mind travels, and I looked forward to them. While under anesthetic for a tonsillectomy at the age of nine, I experienced a reaction to the ether used for the surgery. Again, my body watched from above. This time, I was lying on a wheel much like the one seen on the television show *Wheel of Fortune*. It seemed as if I were from another time and place. The wheel was spinning, and it continued to spin—faster and faster all the while—and I heard a female voice telling me, "You have the power to do anything. It is up to you." In the vision, I was in a white room with a lot of humming vibrations and reverberations.

When I was a child, this type of experience happened all the time. My mother dismissed them as imagination or willfulness. My ability to move my mind out of my body was becoming a common habit, and as I got older, it was perceived as disobedience. I could not convince anyone my visions were real. Were they? I do not know.

The most memorable experience I have ever had occurred when I was nine years old. It happened during prayer at Sunday school class. We were told to close our eyes and cast the devil from our souls. When I closed my eyes, I came face to face with Jesus. I started smiling, and the primary teacher, who I thought looked like the Wicked Witch of the West in *The Wizard of Oz*, yelled at me to stop smiling and to cast the devil from my soul. I told her I saw Jesus, not the devil. She told me it was just the devil trying to fool me. When I closed my eyes again, Jesus was still there, and he told me, "The devil only exists in the minds of man." He told me that people must experience trials and tribulations to learn and that some bad things are given to us so we can learn and grow. He told me that the devil only exists through fear. Jesus smiled at me and winked. It made me smile. At that same moment, my teacher grabbed my arm and jerked me back to reality. She called me a heathen and literally threw me from class, telling me not to come back until I could learn to behave.

I knew then, from the mouth of Jesus, that I was right about what I saw and heard, and my teacher did not understand what I was experiencing. Winking, to this day, is very symbolic to me. I never felt the need to return to organized religion. I love the feeling churches evoke, but my real healing and spirituality comes from my direct, continued connection to Jesus. As I have grown wiser, I realize that the teacher was from the old school of religion, and I was a child who was questioning authority. Sadly, she knew not what she did. She was spiritually blind.

In high school, I worked hard to be a model student and get good grades. I was a cheerleader and homecoming queen, and I was active in competitive sports. I had gained *their* approval. I had all the makings of a perfectionist and overachiever. I was given honor after honor; in fact, my life was perfect until my father passed away when I was seventeen. My perfect world shattered; everything seemed to fall apart. However, I always remembered Jesus' words: "Trials and tribulations happen for growth and learning." However, I did not, at the time, fully understand the meaning.

Unknowingly, the death of my father instilled fear, anger, confusion, abandonment, and a deep sadness in my soul. Without my father, what was going to happen to us—my mom, my little brother, my sister, and me? The fear and worry overwhelmed me. This fear had a significant impact on my psyche and on the way I would choose to live for a very long time to come.

I struggled to do what was expected of me, trying to be strong. At the same time, I was growing wilder and more undisciplined. My perfect world was gone. I became pregnant the summer after my father died, and I got married in the fall, at the age of seventeen. I was thrown out of my senior year of high school for being pregnant. They said I was not a good example to others, and so I was not allowed to continue school.

The approval I had gained was quickly lost. I was humiliated and devastated. My life plan had changed dramatically.

My daughter arrived in the spring, but not without complications. I was under anesthetic because of a difficult delivery, and I underwent another out-of-body experience. I was in a dark tube with a bright light at the end of it. I could see and hear figures standing in the light. As I was moving toward the end of the tube, I heard a woman's voice say, "Your life is changing, and times will be trying; you have a choice to stay in your world or leave and come here with us. But if you choose to live, you will have to fight. You will have to fight to live. Fight to live." As I had learned on the playground, I was going to have to fight to live. I chose to live and jerked out of the anesthetic with a vengeance. It took three nurses to hold me down on the table once I regained consciousness. I was fighting them with everything I had. I wanted to live.

However, the voice was right. My life was changing. My husband and I divorced a few years later. I continued to make one bad decision after another, usually involving drugs, alcohol, and men. I seemed to be everyone's punching bag, including my own. My life seemed to fall into a manic life cycle. Good one minute, unmanageable and depressing the next. I could not find true happiness. Because of my instability, my daughter lived with my mother. As I think back, I am amazed that I am still alive after some of the dangerous stunts I pulled. I was suicidal. I seemed to have a death wish. I took unsafe risks that should have ended my life. Miraculously I survived, maybe to share my story.

Through all this, I still had visions of Jesus reminding me of the trials of life and how one day it would all make sense. I, however, was losing faith in Jesus. I dropped into the depths of despair and fear. He was right. The devil does exist, and he was in my mind. I could not make sense of any of it. I felt so alone. I could not understand why all of this was happening to me.

I no longer trusted myself internally. Externally, I never let them see me sweat. I always appeared to be tough and have it all together. I learned to become angry. My mantra was that I had to "fight to live," and I thought it was working for me. I was a phony.

After years of anger, insecurity, and instability, my spirit guides finally guided me to Salt Lake City, Utah. In the summer of 1988, I went to see a hypnotherapist for weight loss. I knew nothing about the real concept behind how hypnotherapy worked. This is where my journey into the metaphysical sciences began.

The lock to my Pandora's Box or subconscious mind was ready to burst open. My anger, fear, and insecurities could no longer be contained. Hypnotherapy provided a place to let them go. When my emotions finally did burst, all my sadness, loneliness, imperfections, and weaknesses came tumbling out. I could not get Pandora's Box closed again. I felt like Humpty Dumpty—broken into a hundred pieces—and no one could put me together again. I had a nervous breakdown, which actually turned into a breakthrough.

I had been hiding so much of myself from myself and others. The pain, sadness, and resentment of my childhood and adulthood brought me to my knees. From this moment forward, I knew my only path was onward and upward—if I wanted to live.

Through hypnotherapy, I started putting the pieces back into my peace of mind. I found two hypnotherapists I could trust. I called them the good cop and bad cop. The bad cop made me look at my issues of avoidance, and the good cop helped me make sense of them and work through it all. With the help of age regressions and past-life regressions, I started dealing with buried needs of approval, my father's death, the reasons behind the drug and alcohol abuse, and the abysmal hidden secrets in my life. I needed both of these hypnotherapists to help me find the path to peace and understanding.

I was so impressed with them that I studied the hypnotherapy program and became certified as a clinical hypnotherapist in 1991. Thus began my studies in metaphysics, alternative healing, and energy. I figured that if it could help me, it was a magical tool. Please understand, this is not a magic bullet, but a life process and journey. New challenges and impediments occur all the time, testing our strength and faith.

I discovered that I was happiest when I was reading books on energy work, ghosts, or metaphysics. These studies felt familiar to me. These were the things my imaginary friends had showed to me. Since childhood, I had always been able to know things before they happened or feel things that were not there. I have always had visitors in the night—spirits, if you will. Meditation for handling stress was just another word for my astro travel or my out-of-body experiences. The metaphysical world fits me like a glove.

When I was a child, my mother told me, "People with voices in their heads or who see things that aren't really there are put in mental hospitals." Consequently, as I aged, I tried to dismiss the visions, feelings, and voices in my head as craziness. There were women in my family who had ended up in mental hospitals. Mental illness seemed to gallop through my family. However, looking back on my great-aunts, I realize they may have been very intuitive or psychic and did not understand what was happening to them—or maybe they did.

I have discovered through my own experiences that there seems to be a fine line between sanity and insanity, and who is the judge of which one is which? I have noticed in my clients a connection between what has been diagnosed by medical doctors as manic behaviors of depression and anxiety, and increased sensitivity or psychic ability. I believe these people are picking up universal vibrations and, in most cases, do not even realize it. They are comparable to an open lightning rod and become overloaded with energy—sending their bodies into hypermode. The first instinct is to ask, "What is wrong with me?"

Not finding an answer, they trot off to a doctor for a diagnosis and quick fix. I am not saying seeking medical help is wrong, but I believe that more awareness needs to be given to inherent intuitive abilities and environmental sensitivities in addition to medical care. If the two could work together more effectively, the results of treatment would be longer lasting. Take the pill, but also commit to finding out the reasons you may feel the need to take the pill.

As I studied metaphysics, it seemed to enhance my psychic abilities, emotions, and feelings to an all-time high. In one respect, it was very cool, but on another level, it was scary and draining. I did not want to draw criticism and attention to myself, and so I went underground. I had not yet figured out how to come out of my "psychic closet."

One night in a waking sleep, I saw a beautiful woman floating above my bed. She had turquoise-blue eyes and white hair blowing in the wind. She was trying to say something to me, but I could not understand. Needless to say, she scared me and I woke up fast, my heart beating a hundred miles an hour. I had no idea who this woman was and why she was there. I thought that maybe I was possessed or going crazy, just like my great-aunts had done. My religious upbringing did not recognize this as normal behavior; it was classified as the work of the devil. I was not sure who to share this information with, so I mentioned it to no one.

Shortly after my vision, I met an artist who professed to draw spirit guides and guardian angels. Earlier, a psychic had told me that my dad was one of my guides and that he walked frequently with me. I enlisted this artist's services to draw my spirit guide, hoping to get a picture of my father. As she was drawing, I could see it was an image of a woman, not my father. I was very disappointed. I asked if she needed me to be there while she finished the picture and when she said she did not, I left and returned about an hour later. When I walked into the store, beside her chair was a picture of the woman I had seen in my waking-sleep vision. I asked, incredulously, "Who is that?" She answered simply with, "It is your guardian angel." I was speechless. Instantly, I knew this was the woman whose voice I had heard so many years before. I asked her name, but it was not revealed at that time to me.

I felt sorry for this angel, having to follow me around. I do not know how she ever kept me safe. She had some pretty heavy-duty guardian angel assignments taking care of me.

My Guardian Angel

Angelique

From that moment forward, I have never again doubted the power of God, our angels, and our guides. They are the ones who visited me in my childhood and kept me company. They are the ones who talk to me and taught me to mind travel. I felt myself starting to gather hope again. Many years later, through other circumstances, I did learn my angel's name. It is Angelique.

Ironically, after my out-of-body experience in 1972, I wanted to name my new baby daughter Angelique. At the time, Angelique was the name of a vampire on the television soap opera *Dark Shadows*, and members of my family thought the name would have an evil influence on my daughter. I thought it was silly, but I was too young to argue, so I settled for the name Angel Maree. In 1987, still attracted to the name, I legally changed my daughter's name to from Angel to Angelique Maree.

Through a waking dream in 1993, I found out that my guardian angel's name was indeed Angelique. It made sense why I was so attracted to that name after all those years. She was there the day I chose to live.

In retrospect, the reason I chose to live that day was my new baby daughter, Angel. I believe each of us has portal times when we can cross back over to the other side if we choose to do so. The portal was due to open for me at a specific time, and somewhere in my consciousness, I was aware that I would soon be asked to make a choice about whether to stay on Earth or go into the portal. I understand now that this is the reason my body so unexpectedly got pregnant at seventeen, so soon after my father's death.

If the portal had been offered before my daughter's birth, I think I would have made the choice to leave. I felt so disconnected from everything. My daughter saved my life and gave me the hope to live. Angelique was the appropriate name for her as well.

Jesus had told me during this time of darkness that one day my life would all make sense, and he was right. My life purpose was to go on to have a second child, Jessica Montana, and to write my books so that I may help others understand the meaning of life and how everything in our lives truly happens for a reason and at the exact time it is supposed to. As we watch for the signs and metaphors from the heavens, life is indeed a gift.

Needless to say, that day after seeing the picture of my guardian angel, I plunged even deeper into the psychic arts, energy work, and the meaning of life. My life was starting to make sense—piece by piece and peace by peace. The anger was dissipating and peace was surfacing. I continued to look at every modality of healing to keep my body and mind peaceful. I began to read anything on energy that I could get my hands on.

During my hypnotherapy training, the term feng shui, the Chinese art of placement, crept into my vocabulary. I attended a seminar on feng shui and Chinese face reading in Salt Lake City with Lillian Garnier Bridges. At that time, it seemed so foreign. It made little sense, and I seemed to have no frame of reference to apply to it.

However, because everything appears when we need it, shortly afterward I began working with an acupuncturist from Taiwan named Tao Tan, who was helping me with chronic fatigue and Epstein–Barr. Tao told me, "You have bad feng shui." I had no idea what that meant, so I automatically thought he was predicting my doom. He explained it to me, and I realized it was the same concept I had heard from Lillian Bridges during the feng shui seminar. Feng shui was now making sense, and pieces of the puzzle were finally fitting together.

I had noticed that since we had moved into my home in the Salt Lake Valley, my youngest daughter and I had never fully felt healthy. I felt my house made me sick and wondered if it was haunted.

I began to read and apply book feng shui to my house, not really knowing what I was doing. I read, experimented, and read some more. The feng shui books suggested I research the history of my home.

As I researched, I learned that my house was built on what used to be a swamp or river bottom. The Indians crossed this area to get to a fort that once stood nearby. On high water days, many drowned there. I also found out this area was notorious for white settlers' run-ins with the Indians. Unfortunately, my worst fears came true—my house was haunted.

Ultimately, I had an Indian shaman do a blessing on my house. Between the blessing and our remodeling, I was finally able to shift the energy of my home to a place of peace. Feng shui saved my health and sanity. I could truly testify that it works; thus began my career as a feng shui practitioner and a hypnotherapist.

Life continued to throw curves at me. In July 2004, I sustained a serious back injury that affected the mobility of my left leg and foot. A neurosurgeon informed me that there was nothing more the doctors could do for me. The injury was inconclusive on the MRI scan, and we would just have to wait to see how my body would heal. I thought to myself, "What is this 'we' stuff? I am the one who is dealing with this physical affliction."

I had already learned about acupressure and chakras, but now I was going to have to walk my talk. Once again, I immersed myself into a deeper study of how the chakras are affected by the emotions. I began applying feng shui to my environment, getting rid of anything holding me back—those things not allowing me to move forward. I started recording and listening to my own self-hypnosis tapes on healing. My back began to respond and heal.

My foot is still somewhat affected by nerve damage, but for the most part, it is healed. When I start to make a decision that is not right for me, I notice that my foot will start to feel weak and numb. When I remove myself from the situation, it returns to normal. My foot is now my barometer for making decisions.

The mind is powerful and has abilities far beyond what is taught in school. My thought patterns and decisions had considerable control over my body's ability to function and heal. I was a living example of what I believed. Consequently, I began integrating empathic and intuition studies into my feng shui teaching. Thus, my quantum mind program was born.

However, I was still worried about criticism from the powers that be, whoever they were. I second-guessed writing and then publishing this book. Only two people really encouraged me to share my abilities. One was my good cop, hypnotherapist/psychic friend, Betty Finnas. The other was Coni Moyer, a psychic reader. Due to my insecurities and self-doubt, I needed more confirmation.

This mindset led me to Sonia Choquette, a world-renowned psychic. Sonia, in turn, helped me understand that intuitive or psychic abilities should be shared, not hidden. This information should be taught without fear. Unlike my experiences, throughout Sonia's life, many family members and teachers had encouraged her psychic energies. My family and friends discouraged mine. Like Betty and Coni, Sonia encouraged me to begin honoring my visions, voices, and empathic feelings.

I finally understood it. My passions began to come alive. I felt more alive than at any time in my life. I found role models who were not afraid to shout from the rooftops what they do and what they believe. I decided that if they could do it and not be burned at the stake, so could I. As I continued to work on this book, the words just kept coming. I am ready to spread my wings and let others know what I know and see what I see.

When someone asks me what my qualification are to help others, I tell them I have walked the valley of the shadow of death and I have seen the evil while at the same time seeing the light. I understand now why Jesus appeared to me that day many years ago. Without that vision, I would have never understood why my life had to unfold as it has. Jesus was right, my life's trials and tribulations were for a reason. They helped me understand how to help people. I would not be doing what I am doing today without the knowledge of my own experiences and challenges. I draw on those experiences and lessons to help others. I am so happy I was chosen to do this work. It is my passion. This book was meant to be written. It is part of my bigger picture.

I do not care what *they* think anymore. I no longer need *their* approval. I only care what I can do to help others. I am no longer a closet psychic. I am a feng shui practitioner, a hypnotherapist, a spiritual teacher, an energy worker, and I am an intuitive. I AM PSYCHIC! I will help others change their lives in whatever way I can with whatever method I need to use. I am proud of what I do. I will teach others to be proud of who they are and what they do.

I will still experience difficulties. I will still make mistakes. I will still get angry at injustice. I am human—we all are. I have discovered that I may not be perfect in man's eyes, but I am perfect in Jesus' eyes. My faith in Jesus, Buddha, and the power outside of myself is stronger than it has ever been. I have found the innocent nine-year-old again, the girl who trusted the vision to be true and challenged anyone who said it wasn't. The denial of my soul purpose was the lie I was living. It was holding me back. I can't wait to see what the rest of my life holds. I do hope my biggest challenges are behind me, but if they are not, I hope to handle them with grace and ease.

I no longer feel the need to fight to live. I just live. But I still have the instincts. I have a high tolerance to conflict, but can become the cornered cat when pushed past my limit. These limits were established at a very young age. I have a guide who supports this part of me.

He is a Samurai warrior. I have seen him in my visions as well. He looks much like the Ninja Turtle character Shredder. I can't pronounce his name, but he shows up when I am feeling vulnerable. I was guided by him to read the book *Bushido* about the Samurai warriors and their codes.

Helping others find the warrior within their being is also a part of the purpose in my teachings. I want to teach people to stand up for themselves—to find that edge in their personality. Find that passion; find that warrior! We all have one. Each person has this capacity; he or she just needs to find it and defend it.

Sometimes, even though we are not looking, the battle finds us, and we are required to fight for who we are and what we believe. If we don't stick up for our beliefs and ourselves, no one else will. Our behavior may swing from doormat to warrior, but we always swing back to center by using whatever approach is appropriate for us at the right time. Once the pendulum swings back to the center, there is peace, and the feeling of fight or flight lessens.

I tell my clients, "I will support you and give you 110% of me, but only if you are giving yourself 110% dedication. Move your feet and do the work. You can't be a martyr; you can't blame or make excuses. Take responsibility for your decisions and activate involvement in your life's ambitions. If you do not, your life becomes someone else's."

Somewhere in my faith I knew—even as a child—that there was more to my life than most people expected. I have been to China. I am seeing the world. I have met famous people. I still look different and wear unusual clothes. My life is wonderful.

You, too, have the ability to access your dreams. If you can create the visions, you have the power to make them a reality. Challenge yourself. Dream Big. Create. Follow some of the examples in this book and on the accompanying CD. Put them to action. Soar beyond your wildest dreams.

I contribute this book to Jesus, to my guardian angel Angelique, and to my spirit guides. I tell everyone, "Connect to your higher guides. Listen to them; let them guide you." The veil to Heaven is very thin. I know this from personal experience. This book is proof that dreams do come true. It will be an honor serving you. Now, let's get to work manifesting and creating your miracle. I can't wait to hear your story. Thank you for taking time to read this.

Love, Mary

Part ONE

To Balance, You Must Understand

It is so important to find balance in your life. A balance of home, career, self, family, and life. Most importantly, you need to put you in the mix of priorities. This book is committed to unleashing your spirit by balancing the energy of your body, mind, and spirit with the energy of your home and career so that you might rediscover who you really are. This book incorporates hypnotherapy, feng shui, and other metaphysical tools to help you accomplish your goals.

People ask me all the time, "What do you mean when you say energy?"

Energy is what we do or don't have when we wake up in the morning. It is what takes us through the day. It is what serves us and helps us be more productive. It could be food, music, a comfortable chair, or even another person. It will be different with everyone. Energy is the vibration field, also called the energetic field or aura field, surrounding every living thing as well as inanimate objects. Some things in our environment help us feel healthier and more productive, while others literally suck our energy. It is of vital importance to open our feng shui eyes and learn what does or doesn't support our well-being.

As I developed my feng shui ability, the first skill I needed to perfect was my power of observation and awareness. I had to hone my body to tune in to every energy in a room. My mind and body learned to scan my environment and focus on those things not in keeping with my energy field. I call what I do "quantum feng shui." Quantum means taking a jump into the inner working of the mind and feelings, and trusting my inner voice, feelings, and vibes to quickly pinpoint energy or objects that can be a disruption to the harmony of the body, mind, and spirit.

I have spent considerable time reading, studying, and researching the fields of physics and metaphysics. I realized that feng shui is actually a form of quantum physics in which many forms of energy are subdivided in smaller increments.

Feng shui is Mandarin Chinese for "wind and water." Because the language is very simple, interpreted it simply means movement of energy, chi, or life force—your life force. Feng shui can be representative of both physics and metaphysics.

Basic feng shui is comparable to physics. Physics, according to *Webster*, is the study of a natural science dealing with matter and energy and its interaction in the fields of mechanics, sound, optics, heat, electricity, magnetism, radiation, atomic structure, and nuclear phenomena; thus, feng shui deals with interaction of energy and the effect upon the human body.

Esoteric feng shui can be considered a branch of philosophy and metaphysics. Philosophy is the pursuit of wisdom, a search for greater understanding by speculative and observation means. Philosophy is concerned with explaining the ultimate nature of being and the world. In addition, esoteric or spiritual feng shui focuses on manifesting the power of thought and the spoken word and how they impact our existence. This spiritual aspect of feng shui is very important because it forms our very being. It strives to understand the workings of life's purpose—the Tao.

Metaphysics is essentially the energy of the Earth and the energy of the human body that interacts together in an orderly manner. Within metaphysics, we have divisions of cosmology and ontology.

Cosmology is the study of the universe and humanity's place in it. The study of the universe has a long history involving science, philosophy, esotericism, and religion—

feng shui. Cosmology deals with origin, structure, and the space–time relationship of the universe. Flying Stars feng shui may be put into this division.

Ontology is the study of the nature of being or existence and its relations to others and self. Ontology deals with questions concerning what can be seen to exist and what is thought to exist.

In essence, feng shui is the art of placement, which deals with our interaction within our environment. The only thing separating physics and metaphysics and feng shui is semantics. In essence, they are the same thing—that which can be seen and unseen but that affects our reality.

Quantum Mind Feng Shui combines all the above and helps us tune into the inner mind, understand the vibrations and energy around us, and realign ourselves with those frequencies. As we clear and reconstruct positive energy in our environment, the outcome is a more positive, healthy, content life, no matter what destiny throws at us.

If you are a beginning student of metaphysics, feng shui, and self-hypnosis methods, or if you just want to increase your psychic awareness, it is important to know that you are required to tune into your senses. You must allow yourself to see what the eye cannot see, hear what is not being said, and feel what needs to be felt. The human body is your radar antenna, and if you develop your power of awareness and observation, your body will guide you easily in quantum mind awareness.

To get the most from this book and Quantum Mind Feng Shui, you must realize that this book is a creative guide to teach new ideas to help you create your own life. My job is to deliver the message. Your job is to receive it and create from it. Your career, from this point forward, is that of an artist. The canvas is blank to create and keep creating—whatever it is you wish to build. Make your dreams a projected reality using intuition, goal setting, and commitment. This book teaches you to move from patriarchal intellectualism to matriarchal intuition—and then to create a balance between the two, completing your being.

Intellectualism is based in calculations, facts, and numbers. Intuition is based on the moment in time, energy, and movement. Remember, this moment is gone and the next has approached and the next is approaching. The facts and calculations of the last moment are gone, never to be retrieved, so why sweat our intuitive ability to justify the past, the future, or the present? Don't get manipulated into a standoff with intellect vs. intuition.

There is not an intellectual higher learning institute that recognizes intuition or psychic ability as a valid art degree. Quantum physics is as close as we get. I have a premonition that the time is coming very soon that it will be acknowledged. Consequently, until then, we must recognize that ability within ourselves.

Learn to trust your instincts, your hunches, and your gut. Trust your intuition. You decide what is good for you from a deeper level in your cells. Don't allow *them* to make your decisions or paint your canvas. Because after all, who are *they* anyway?

Let your body start being your compass. Start paying attention to what your body is trying to tell you. Is your heart beating rapidly? Are you sweating? Do you suddenly feel headachy or sick to your stomach? Or does it feel calm, serene, and just right? Become alert when your body talks. As you develop your sixth sense, trust yourself to know what is right for you, your home, and your family.

Feng shui energy is ever changing based upon the personal interaction of your body and your environment. Learn to recognize these changes, signs, metaphors, and meanings of things occurring in your life. Put the signs to work in your favor. Look for symbols. Don't allow scotoma, the partial loss of vision or a blind spot in your vision or perception, to set in. Pay attention to your senses and to all aspects of your environment.

Start paying attention to your environment and the people with whom you associate. Watch their body language, their eyes, and their hands. Which way are they looking or pointing as they are speaking? Their body will tell you the story of truth. Use these guides to develop your extrasensory feelings. It is your natural ability. You were born with it. Use it appropriately.

Keep an open mind and honor the mysterious energy that governs the Earth, the atmosphere, and all life forms, especially humans. This energy encompasses the mind, body, and spirit of all living things. Realize there are no accidents, no mistakes, and no chances. Everything is a destiny meeting, and everyone is in your life for a reason. Learn to allow destiny to unfold. Look for the mystery. Look for the signs.

Start paying attention to the bioenergetics of your feng shui. Simply put, this is how you and other living things interact within your environment. These interactions affect your ability to learn, your ability to prosper, and your ability to manifest. Look for the positive in all aspects of your life. Let go or disconnect from all things that bring you discontentment, unhappiness, or stress. As you will find in this book, our body holds memories that are connected to certain objects, smells, places, and people. It is important to cut the cord to these things to achieve a new level of learning. Letting go is really easier than you believe. De-clutter. Say "bye-bye," and don't look back.

Understand that feng shui is not a cure for all your problems. Feng shui, when adjusted properly, helps you understand and cope with anything that may make you uncomfortable. It is a learning experience. Explore the Earth's energy that radiates from the eight directions and from the Earth's surface, creating auspicious and inauspicious circumstances in your existence that can bring harmony to your mind, body, and spirit. As understanding develops, inauspicious circumstances or problems become smaller and less important.

Internal and external feng shui increases your environmental awareness. Your external environment affects your internal well-being of the mind and body and vice versa. Internal feng shui can be a holistic approach to the improvement of the mind, body, and spirit. Remember, your environment is an extension of your mind. If you wish to change your behavior and goals, change your environment. It may be the cause of the problem. For example, recovering alcoholics can no longer hang out with old friends at the local pub or sit in their drinking chair at home. They must find new friends and a new playground if they wish to manifest change.

Spiritual feng shui regards spirituality but is not a specific religion. You must believe in something, whether it is God, Jesus, Buddha, Great Spirit, Nature, or the higher power of self. Honor the Heaven, the Earth, and man's connection to it. This connection can serve to make your personal religious beliefs even stronger.

Black Hat Feng Shui, even though based on the Taoist text, can be applied universally to any religion. If the traditional Buddhist/Taoist feng shui mantra, mudra, or prayer makes you uncomfortable, adapt it to fit your own belief system. Don't let religion or society get in the way of your beliefs. Use common sense and not fear when it comes to applying and adapting feng shui principles to fit into your Western world and your religion. Make your world of feng shui your own. Use your personal verbiage, spiritual prayer, mantra, mudra, and symbolism to help accomplish this. Your inner spirit will help you make the right adjustments.

Every thought is a self-prophecy. What you think, you will become. Remember, thoughts spring forward into action. The Holy Bible and other religious texts carry many passages referring to the power of the spoken word and the ways in which these words can contribute to our life or our death.

Complete the following sentence. Don't be limited in your thinking; be creative.

If I could do or be anything in the world, I would ______________________________.

If negative energy should creep into your mind, cross out all opposing thoughts as soon as they occur and replace them with three positive thoughts. Meditate or pray for intuition and guidance, and allow the rest to just flow with nature.

Be willing to take the risk that something marvelous may happen to you. For example, you have picked up this book for a reason. From this minute forward, pay attention to all the wonderful things that are changing in your life. Look for those little gifts of abundance and happiness that land in your path. Some things may come easier than others, but appreciate it all—everything has a season and a reason.

Ask questions and search out new books and teacher's opinions on feng shui, energy modalities, and personal growth. There are so many terrific teachers out there—some known and others unknown. Each teacher will have a different teaching method or viewpoint. Each may hold a piece of your puzzle. You must learn the basic rules of quantum mind feng shui before you can break them. Feng shui has basic guides to follow, but remember, so much of feng shui is intuitive. Each teacher's opinion should always be honored as his or her perspective. This is what makes feng shui ever changing.

The biggest misnomer in the feng shui adjustment world is that one cure will work the same way for everyone. No single or individual cure is set in stone. Energy adjustments are based on individual body reactions to the environment. Be willing to investigate and document your research and make necessary adjustments when adjustment is needed, even if it does not seem to follow the norm of feng shui. A situation will change from minute to minute, and what you see now may not be what someone else saw five minutes before you. Remember to honor those changes in yourself and others. If you only learn one important lesson from your teacher, you have gained a great gift.

Teachers come in all sizes, shapes, experiences, and ages. Be willing to learn from each. In part, that is what makes feng shui so incredible.

Be in the NOW. Don't look back; that is the past. Don't live in the future or you miss the gifts of the now. Bless what you have now, not what you hope to attain in the future. It will all come in due time at the exact moment it is supposed to. Cherish each moment as it is happening. Use all of your senses. Smell more flowers, touch more lives, see more of nature's beauty, and hear what is not being said. This is where the now is. If the moment is not making you happy, adjust your moment or your mind paradigm.

You have the power to control your life and who or what is in it. Take charge of your life, but allow your destiny to unfold naturally. Don't try to make it unfold. If it is supposed to happen, it will. The universe just waits for you to make the decision that you desire good things in your life.

Take responsibility for your attitude and actions. Let others take responsibility for theirs. For every action, there is a reaction. Remember, you are creating your own karma. It is the tai chi or circle of life. What you put out will be returned tenfold—so make sure you are putting out those things you want in return.

Be humble and grateful for your life. Show gratitude every day for the blessings in your life, good or bad. Each aspect of our lives is a blessing in disguise. As you meditate, show gratitude and practice patience. Meditate every day for answers to everyday situations.

Expect a miracle. It can happen to you and for you. Get clear on your dreams and whether they are doable. Understand that some projects may need to be tweaked and re-tweaked, then scrapped and re-tweaked again before they manifest. Some dreams may not manifest the way we envisioned, but manifest better. It doesn't matter, as long as the commitment results in victory.

Don't give up on your dreams. If you can dream it, you can be it. You have the responsibility to make it happen. If God gave you the idea, he will also give you a way to manifest it. Intuition is the map to aspire us to higher levels of dreams. Intuition gives you guidance. Walt Disney was considered crazy, and Albert Einstein was considered eccentric, and they both achieved great things. They accomplished them outside of the conventional way things were done. Rock on and roll forward. Your life is waiting.

Quantum Mind Feng Shui incorporates a broadband of information. The program incorporates the chakras of the body, identifying and pinpointing areas of concern and steps to correct them. It embodies feng shui, which works with the earth a home sits upon, the physical structure of the exterior and interior of the home, and the interaction of the physical, emotional, and spiritual levels of your body and its relationship with the interior of the home. Feng shui, on an esoteric level, may help pinpoint the reasons why a behavior or phenomenon is occurring in your life. The program is enhanced or empowered with self-hypnosis and goal setting.

You must always be clear on your intentions. You do not get in a taxicab and tell the driver, "I don't want to go to the airport or the hospital or the hotel." You tell the driver exactly where you wish to go, and you have expectations of arriving there within a designated time frame. That is how our mind works. If you are not sure where you are going or what your goals are, you will not arrive where you would like to go.

Too many distractions or too much clutter in the home or mind can be detrimental to accomplishing your goals. Learn to use the external environment of your home or business to visually accent and uplift your heart's desire.

Use meditation skills or self-hypnosis methods to set this behavior and open the mind to the cosmic or psychic power of the source of the universe, God. Then sit back and watch your goals and dreams begin to manifest more quickly than you thought possible.

Everyone is blessed with the sixth-sensory ability; some just seem to be more aware and sensitive to it. To assist psychic awareness, growth, and development, use the exercises and methods in this book to help make the necessary changes easier and more effective. This shift may not always be an easy one, but it will be worth it. It is important to ground your body and mind and to develop the quantum mindset of leaping into conscious awareness and manifesting what is needed and required.

With these thoughts in mind, proceed and learn the basics of quantum mind feng shui spelled out in a mind, body, and spirit connection—and discover how you can improve the quality of your life.

Everyone has a different approach to the way he or she views life and ambitions. Decide which category you may fall into, and make a decision about the necessary adjustments you may need to make to achieve your desired changes.

Some people know exactly what they want out of life and go after it, no matter what it takes. They have focused their goals and succeeded at fulfilling them. They are usually successful and high profile. They may ride a fine line between overachievement and happiness.

Overachievers are always busy—mentally and physically—completing one project after another, taking on more than they can handle. They allow little or no time for rest and relaxation. Overachievers usually want it all and want to experience it all. They can become stressed out easily and find no joy in the fast process even though it is their heart's desire to experience it all.

These people need to slow down, complete, and enjoy their desires one step at a time. Life does not need to be a destination, but instead is a journey. Realize that you have your entire life to complete the adventure. Life and learning does not end at a certain age. It ends because one quits thinking, learning, and looking to the future. Remember to keep dancing, laughing, and playing—no matter what age you are. All your desires can be completed within your lifetime. It is okay to grow, change, or adjust your desire. Slow down and hear your laughter. The journey should be one of joy.

On the other end of the spectrum, we may see those individuals who have no goals and do not want any. That is their goal. They choose to remain uncommitted to anything. Many live very simple, happy lives doing this. If it works for them, it is okay.

However, within this group, we may see those who are truly lost or confused about what they want to do with their life, and they wish someone would figure it out for them. They want someone else to tell them what to do and how to do it. These individuals need to get clear on what they want to achieve in the lifetime and then determine steps to make it happen. Making a list of their hopes and dreams helps to set a plan in motion. Once set into motion, it can become a reality.

The people pleasers or caretakers have the toughest job. These individuals live their lives taking care of or pleasing others without asking for what they need in return to be happy. They live vicariously through others. They do what they think is expected of them in exchange for praise or approval. They stay so distracted by other people's needs (family, children, friends, parents, etc.) that they don't focus on their own needs. They define their lives through others' accomplishments. Their spirits are soon depleted because they feel unfulfilled, with no accomplishments of their own.

Unfortunately, sometimes we all may have little choice but to take care of children or an aging parent. It is important that you find a balance between your personal needs and those of others. It may be up to you to teach those you are taking care of when to be dependent, independent, and/or interdependent upon each other.

Caretakers, as they become exhausted, may grow nervous, overweight, sluggish, unhappy, controlling, or martyr-like. In extreme cases, they may develop higher incidences of medically diagnosed illnesses such as depression, chronic fatigue, some cancers, or addictions. Since others' needs are usually first and foremost to the caretaker, his or her own health is neglected.

Author Louise Hay has a wonderful book entitled *Heal Your Body*, which is about the emotional causes of physical illness and the metaphysical way to overcome them. I highly recommend this book to anyone who has frequent and chronic aches and pains. After reading Hay's book in 1989, and with the help of feng shui and hypnotherapy, I experienced a real sense of being whole for the first time since childhood. My life changed dramatically. I began to understand my own life experiences, my own thought patterns, and my own psychic abilities. I was able to begin connecting my mental health with my physical health—my mind, body, spirit connection.

Understanding my own people-pleaser aspect enabled me to understand I was not ill, crazy, or possessed by the devil. I learned to balance others and myself. Today, I am healthy, happy, and whole. I still take care of my family, friends, and clients, but I also take care of myself.

Life still presents challenges, which I must deal with daily, but they are no longer incapacitating. Awareness is the key to setting boundaries and overcoming adversity. I am blessed by God with the gift of intuition, and I now understand how to use it. My body is my radar tool. I pay attention when I begin taking on too much stress or have too many toxic situations. I simply remove myself from the situation and take a break. This downtime helps keep the physical challenges at bay and my intuitive abilities clear. Downtime is freeing and necessary.

In Chinese medicine and acupuncture, a Chinese doctor will look at all aspects of the mind, body, and spirit to obtain a diagnosis of the health of a body. Some look to the land and environment of the patient for answers as well. A Chinese doctor will usually tell his/her clients to "take rest" when faced with illness.

A feng shui practitioner becomes somewhat of a house doctor, looking at the mind, body, and the spirit of the home. We consider the land, climate, and environment and then adjust the home's external and internal factors to fit the occupants of the space. However, we are not medical doctors, and this book is not to substitute for any medical treatment you are receiving or should receive.

The purpose of this book is to serve as a reference guide of compiled research—at your fingertips—and includes different areas of energy work employing mundane and esoteric feng shui methods and self-hypnosis meditations for personal understanding and growth. This book is a tool to be used to provoke thought so that physical changes may be made, resulting in a more harmonious existence. Change cannot occur without thought and active movement or action to make it happen. I call this "shaking up your chi."

Common sense tells us that we—as living things—were produced from the matter of the five elements of the Earth when the Earth was created: water, wood (air), fire, earth, and metal (mineral). In religious texts, the Christian or Western religious traditions believe that God created Earth and man, and the Eastern traditions of Buddhism and Taoism believe God and nature are one in the same, as stated in the Book of I Ching, thus making this Heaven on Earth. The difference in philosophies seems to be a question of semantics more than substance. Both seem to be saying somewhat the same thing, and the final analysis is left up to the individual to interpret. The real question is how we make Heaven on Earth and live in harmony while dealing with all the trials and tribulations we face in our everyday lives. It is said, "It does not matter what happens to us, but how we choose to react to it is what matters."

I ask you now to contemplate the following questions and then examine how they directly affect your life's physical, spiritual, and mental well-being.

How can you, as one person, begin making changes in your life to invoke positive changes for our world?

What environmental changes have been occurring on the Earth's surface and to its resources within the last one hundred years, and what effect have they had on humankind and the ecosystem?

Why is there a need for more and more material objects and competition to make our lives feel more complete?

In the many tribes of man, why does there seem to be a lack of balance of emotions and behaviors, such as the increase of aggression and abuse toward each other compounded by the increase of drug and alcohol abuse? Even the animal kingdom is showing more signs of aggression.

Finally, where is the empathy and love for fellow man? What has happened to peace on Earth?

Could the reason for this list of changes be that nature and its spirit are no longer a major part of our lives? With the advent of modern amenities, have we disconnected from nature? Are we a throwaway generation? Think about the role of nature and how all of its elements play in our lives.

Until the 1900s, people spent most of their time outdoors, working, gardening, walking, or just spending time with each other in recreational sports. In the 1990s, people spent most of their time indoors, either working, sitting at the computer, watching TV, or watching recreational sports inside a building. Think about it: a car ride vs. a hike, a computer game vs. a neighborhood baseball game, driving vs. walking. Our lifestyles have changed dramatically—from outdoors to indoors, and from activity to inactivity. I don't see any indication that this change will return to what it was any time soon.

In my experiences as a practitioner, I have seen and felt a disconnection of humankind from nature as well as a blatant lack of respect for the Earth and its natural resources. Personally, I believe this disconnect may be causing some of the upset in our society today. Nature connects us to the Earth and to each other as well; it acts as the lightning rod that binds us together as one. I believe this disconnect and insolence is due to our chosen busy lifestyles, a lack of knowledge or caring for the ecosystem and its functions in relation to living things, and our quality of life.

Grand Master Professor Lin Yun says the Internet is a way people are isolating themselves from society and disconnecting with the physical. As we shop and entertain ourselves on the Internet, the personal contact we need drops, and society becomes apathetic or antisocial. As man becomes unconcerned, emotions shut down, and disharmonies with the natural rhythms of the body prevail.

Feng shui may be a partial answer to these problems. It helps solve, resolve, and relieve some of the stresses our everyday lives create by reconnecting us with the elements of nature. Feng shui can help bring the elements of nature back into balance within the home and body, creating a private sanctuary with a natural feel. As we learn to balance out and pay attention to the elements of nature within our homes or businesses, we balance out our inner feng shui as well.

Go to the mountains or the ocean and notice the automatic shift in your attitude. Watch your children as they play in the mountains or by the water, and compare it to how they play at home. Make a journal and pay attention to it. You will find that children play harder, laugh more, and tend to get tired at sunset—as nature intended. In the mountains, for instance, notice how everyone gets up with the sun. It is hard to sleep when the sun is coming up on the body. As the morning sun shines on our bodies, it activates the chi to cause us to want to shake our booties!

This awareness of our inner feng shui or esoteric feng shui in turn truly connects us to our source: God, Nature, Spirit, or whatever name your belief system wishes to use. Dawn McKenzie, in her book *Heart Warmers*, says, "Whatever controls your life can be defined as a religion." Remember to apply your religious beliefs to your feng shui. In turn, this brings our lives back to harmony and peace. Thus, the stress level decreases, lessening the chance of disease.

Quality of life is directly proportional to and determined by the quality of life one experiences at home. During the years I practiced only hypnotherapy, I noticed that people were able to make significant changes while sitting in my office. By the next week, though, they would have fallen back into some of the old behaviors, comfortable with "just being—too tired to make the changes." I realized that the stale home or business environment could cause a "tired chi." Tired chi is caused by tired or stressed routines that develop within homes and workplaces.

This environmental influence, in addition to the weight of past conditioning of the mind (emotional feng shui), may be blocking the ability to change a behavior. As with any living species, everything has a pecking order, and sometimes the pecking order within the home or business is established nonverbally, by the positions of chairs in a room, pictures on the walls, and maybe even the clothes or hairstyles we wear. Even a color, a smell, or the energy or memory of an object could be sending a message to the subconscious mind, triggering self-esteem issues held onto from the past, making it a struggle to get past this conditioning.

It becomes extremely important to alter the trigger. A trigger is a reaction to a specific person, place, or thing that stimulates emotions—good or bad—within the home. By using a combination of feng shui and self-hypnosis methods to shake up the routine, change is achieved.

The mind is composed of the conscious and subconscious. The subconscious mind is our autopilot, and the behaviors to protect us were formed when we were young. We drew on those impressions of protection when we felt frightened or had the need for security and acceptance. As we age, those same mechanisms are still set in stone and influence our behavior. Our home and body reflect these beliefs.

As children, we start out happy and innocent and then judgments and thumbprints, put upon our subconscious mind by our mentors or peers, begin to block our true reasoning of self, clarity of mindful thinking, and most importantly, our image of self. Feng shui energy work, in combination with self-hypnosis and self-awareness conditioning, can help resolve whatever stumbling blocks are standing in the way of having the complete happy life we deserve. This method can take us full circle, back to a beginning of time when we possessed a very complete and happy life.

Experts agree that we only use ten percent of our mind. What, then, is in the other ninety percent? The mind takes in millions of messages through its senses every day, but it is only able to process a few thousand of them. So what happens to the rest of the messages? I personally believe they are stored in the other ninety percent of the brain's memory to be processed for future use. Through meditation and awareness, we are able to access daily, for our use, these memories. We are able to leap forward in consciousness and rise above the mental capability man believes he can achieve. This quantum mind thinking allows us the ability to truly trust our intuition, hunches, and vibes and gain information from the past and future.

As I gained experience incorporating feng shui with behavior modification, it became apparent how important it is to understand the underlying messages our homes are sending us. Every item in our home literally holds a message for the senses of sight, smell, taste, touch, hearing, and of course the sixth sense of knowing—the unseen feeling of pleasure or foreboding. As a feng shui practitioner, it became my job to literally step into every clients' body, mind, and spirit to understand what they were experiencing within their lives through their emotions and their thoughts; thus, *Quantum Mind Feng Shui* was born.

I found that even the simplest changes in the home or business—perhaps a color scheme change, changes in the placement of furniture, or changing the pictures on the wall—would facilitate huge realignment of spirit within a home and in behavior. On a personal level, this may include getting a new hairstyle, new clothes, or even a new job. Change from the same old routine breathes new chi into the home or body. This is why we love to shop. It isn't because we love to spend money or are materialists, it is because we grow tired of the old chi (old items) and need new chi (new items) to revitalize. We are literally breathing new life into ourselves.

Once we understand what is lacking in our lives or environment, we are then able to adjust, replace, and improve our lives as we let the stress roll off our backs. Stress has been proven to be the precursor of diseases such as cancer, chronic fatigue, asthma, multiple sclerosis, and others, so it is important to make the changes necessary to restore optimum health. What are you willing to do to help reach your fullest potential for your mind, body, and spirit?

Subconsciously, our body can also feel the effects of geopathic or electromagnetic stresses that run through or under a home or business. These stresses may also affect the quality of life within the home. Electomagnetic radiation may affect the nervous system. This influence may increase emotions and frustrations. Electric and magnetic fields (EMFs) can cause a simple situation to become blown out of proportion or an already intense situation to become volatile. Children may develop hyperactivity and sleep disorders from the added energy.

Dowsing, pendulums, or gauss meter work is used to help identify these environmental areas. Everyone needs to become more aware of stress areas in his or her environment and then seek out ways to correct them. The result will be a healthier living place—one that better supports our bodies. As we bring balance and healing into our own lives, we restore balance and healing to our other Earth home—mother Earth.

As we become more in tune with our natural psychic abilities, we know what we need to do with our lives and environment to find balance. We can't change the world, but we can change things in our world, one thing at a time and one person at a time. We can be the change we hope to see.

Life becomes a "pay it forward" situation. As someone teaches you something worthwhile or performs a random act of kindness for you, it becomes your responsibility to go out and teach something worthwhile or perform a random act of kindness for two to ten other people. As you teach and learn these lessons, you will find that the world does start changing, and it can start changing right now for you.

As an interior design–feng shui practitioner/hypnotherapist, I see specific situations in people's lives that really make me scratch my head and wonder, "What is the meaning of life, and why does this happen?" Sometimes bad things happen to good people. As I see the many depths of life and its occurrences and lessons, it makes me realize that the more I know, the less I feel I know about life and the energy that governs us. I have come to understand that my learning and continuing education will never end. I will keep striving to make this world a better place in which to live. Please help me to do this. Together, we will make the difference we all desire.

Peace be with you, and I hope you enjoy the research that I—and many who have come before me—have done to make this book possible for you. Take what fits you, and throw the rest away or tweak it to fit your lifestyle.

Believe nothing, no matter where you read it, or who said it,
no matter if I have said it, unless it agrees with your own reason
and your own common sense.

Quote from the Master Teacher—Buddha

Part

TWO

Defining Feng Shui

Feng shui does for the home what acupuncture does for the body.

Feng shui (pronounced fung schway) is an ancient art of placement derived from the belief that unique, mysterious, and unseen Earth energy forces interact with our surroundings, creating harmony or disharmony depending on the specifics of the interaction. Feng shui deals with three levels of energy affecting the human body: physical, mental, and spiritual. It is an eco art dealing with conservation, ecology, orientation, spatial arrangements, and interior design. When one aspect of the body is out of sync, all areas are affected. This is why it is so important to understand the physical aspect of our existence before we can understand and access the quantum mind theories of our existence.

Understanding the basics of feng shui and your physical environment will help stabilize the chakras of the body so the mind can access and process the information that goes into its super consciousness. As the body and mind are at peace, truth and clarity are seen. We begin to trust the higher vibration level and are more able to access information from the Cosmos/God.

The Cosmos is a source outside the body that gives information to humankind daily. Cosmos may also be referred to as God, Jesus, Buddha, higher self, angelic beings, spirit guides, deceased relatives, or whatever—Yoda if you wish.

When the body is in perfect alignment, this information is delivered at the exact moment in time that it is to be received, and the information is trusted and executed without doubt. Peace, unconditional love, and happiness are achieved on Earth. As mentioned before, this is not a cure-all for pain and suffering; it is a tool to help us understand life's process. We are programmed to receive only pieces of the puzzle. If you were able to receive all the puzzle pieces at once, there would be no purpose for life and learning. This is the game of life. Play it for fun, and do not take it too seriously because tomorrow all will change anyway. It will all be revealed upon our death. Try not to rush the process.

The environment of your home can affect your ability to receive these messages. If you live in a cluttered, stale environment, the mind is too busy processing the junk through your senses, and it is not able to focus on growing or living life to its fullest. This is why conscious environmental awareness is so important, and the depths of feng shui are explored and understood.

A Scientific Look at Feng Shui

Many, from the beginning of time and among many world cultures, have acknowledged energy work. On the physical level of feng shui, geomancers believe the Earth is alive and breathing, and all that inhabits the Earth are bioenergetics. Geomancers study the biology of energy transformations and energy exchanges within and between living things and the environment. In 1937, a man named Peyre began talking about a geomagnetic net covering the Earth. By 1942, it was documented that this theoretical net indeed did exist and was formed from an interaction of the magnetism from the sun and the magnetism of the Earth. Nightfall created a slight shift in the net, causing the tides and the human emotions to ebb and flow, thus giving validity to the theory of the Earth's "breathing."

The small Peyre nets, named after the man who studied them, were divided into three parts. The nets run north and south, east and west, and at the point where the energy net interlaces and crosses, creating a square. Incredibly, this square resembles the Lo-Shu/ba gua square of feng shui.

When a contamination of the Peyre net occurs, a Hartmann net is formed. The contaminations are caused by the negative electromagnetic or geopathic energy of the Earth. When this occurs, the Hartmann net forms as a resonance that extends in the north-to-south and in the east-to-west directions, which cross over the top of the smaller Peyre nets. When man-made electromagnetism becomes involved, these nets become very harmful to the body. Old Chinese text calls these geopathic zones "the exit of evil" and the Chinese, as early as 4000 BC, called these energy nets feng shui.

The study of the Earth's magnetic field has a long and illustrious history throughout world cultures. According to the legends of Atlantis, when all the continents' masses were joined, cultures practiced similar methods of mathematics, astrology, and spiritual ceremonies. When Atlantis sank due to catastrophic tectonic activity and the continents separated, the information practices of all of the cultures—although now separated—remained intact.

Those who escaped the cataclysm—the Mayans of Mexico and South America, the Chinese and Hindu in Eastern Asia, the Romans, the Celts and Druids in Ireland, the Egyptians, and the Native Americans in the Americas—continued to develop their ideas, traditions, and trades on what would now be different continents. This could be one of the explanations for the similarities in scientific and mystical phenomena of cultures around the world, separated by vast oceans, during a time when the only travel between continents was by boat.

These cultures combined science (alchemy) and spiritual intention. They used "seers" or those with the "gift of prophecy" to lead to some of the discoveries that are the foundations of science to this day. However, the vortex energies around Stonehenge, the Pyramids, the Bermuda Triangle, and numerous other sites around the world remain a mystery today. Modern-day energy practitioners are studying and documenting the physical effects these and other vortexes have on the life forms that come into contact with them. This interaction is called bioenergetics or feng shui.

Bioenergetics is the study of the transformation of energy in living organisms. The bioenergetics of all living things on the Earth will inherently seek to balance all bio-environmental factors. Hippocrates, the father of Western medicine (460 to 377 BC), maintained that the body has the natural capacity to heal itself, and it will automatically—on some level in the mind, body, or spirit—search for the adjustments needed to restore and maintain perfect health. He challenged medical superstitions and replaced them with scientific observations. He used diet, fresh air, physical exercise, medicinal waters, and the healing tendency of nature. According to the Hippocratic Collection,

The Airs, Waters, and Places, the nucleus of writings ascribed to Hippocrates, was the first dissertation on climatology. Its basic premise is that the human body is not separate from nature but a part of the energetic inner weaving of all life of all things. Thus, an old term, thousands of years old, becomes scientific. This old term is feng shui.

The feng shui energy or bioenergetic energy from this point on will be referred to as "chi" or "qi." Chi or qi is considered the breath, prana, or life force that breathes vital energy into and throughout our bodies and our environment. When disharmony or disease strikes, it is thought to be a disruption of the energy flow into a vessel, whether it is the body or the home.

The Earth energy level of feng shui encompasses the grounding and stability of our life upon the topography of the Earth. It is our actual association with the Earth's surface and the effect it has upon the human body. Scientists have studied for centuries such aspects as the Earth's gravity, its association with the magnetic movement of the four directions, and the pressure it exerts per square inch on the Earth's surface. These conditions of atmospheric pressure have been associated with headaches and joint pain for decades. The moon cycles in conjunction with the tides have been proven to coincide with the well-being of the emotional state of mind. Studies have shown that emergency rooms are usually busier during a full moon cycle. Animals tend to become more ill at ease and tend to pace or prowl more during the full moon as well.

In modern times, feng shui on a conscious level is used to bring the qi of living spaces into harmony with the people who live and work there. The art of feng shui helps us recognize energy patterns and changes within our environment and then teaches us how to adjust them.

Our external environment affects our internal state of being and vice versa. Feng shui teaches environmental consciousness—learning to become aware of harmony or disharmony within our space, and thus correcting it. Feng shui helps us use our home and business to nurture and support our well-being.

On an emotional or mental level, the nature of a building or home where we live has a direct effect on the way we feel about ourselves and influences our communication with others. Our ideas, personalities, and emotions are expressed through the design of our home. Design of the home includes anything within the home that has a particular purpose. Our home becomes the communicator or self-portrait to others. As we communicate through design, we become what we see. This gives credibility to the statement, "What you see is what you get."

If you wake in the morning and your home is pleasing to the eye, with attractive colors and items that you love, your day will likely be good. However, if you awake in the morning to a sink of dirty dishes, a cluttered home, or a home with distracting colors, chances are your day will not get any better.

Feng shui on a spiritual level has to do with manifesting the "power of thought or the spoken word." The spiritual level of feng shui is very important in our lives, as it can form and affect our very being. This is the esoteric or mystical feng shui that can change your life.

The most difficult part of feng shui is to understand the four-pillar Eastern astrology and the Flying Stars feng shui and how they interact with each other. It is so important when learning feng shui to know what your personal body energy element makeup or inner feng shui makeup is. This profile is called the four-pillar destiny. It is your heavenly energy determined by the time and location of your birth. The four-pillar profile can pinpoint exactly what earth elements and their percentages were present at the time of your birth.

Once the personal chi elements of the body are discovered, we can begin to create a harmonious living space for that individual. It is important to understand how the elements of the universe work. Balancing the elements of the universe is one of the most important aspects of feng shui. When you are balanced with your elements, harmony and peace will instinctively follow. There are many great books on the four-pillar destiny profile. The four-pillar profiles are complicated but definitely worth the time to explore and learn. I recommend hiring a qualified practitioner to ensure the charts are accurate. Charts are also available at www.maryshurtleff.com.

Those proficient in the compass method of feng shui have a process called the "flying stars" to determine how the home affects our harmony. The Flying Stars feng shui is based on ancient calculations of astronomy, navigation, and mathematics. This method is thousands of years old. The flying stars method is used to determine how the energies of the Earth and its directions from different time periods affect our lives and well-being.

The flying stars of a home or business are determined by the year and the period it was built and the direction the home is facing; then an added dimension of the annual flying stars is incorporated. Each star has a specific significance, and the stars are then compared to determine function.

I recommend taking a class from a qualified teacher or hiring a qualified practitioner to teach you the proper techniques for the flying stars. Ask for credentials. The flying stars are confusing, but once understood, they are invaluable.

The Different Schools of Feng Shui

Land Form Feng Shui

Feng shui is an art of placement translated by many masters who practiced and mastered their environments. There are three prominent schools of feng shui: the Landform School, the Compass School, and the Black Hat Sect School. Within each school are numerous other schools of feng shui. Each has its own history, but all schools have validity in helping one understand his/her environment. More and more practitioners are trying to integrate all the schools of feng shui into their studies to understand better the mysterious energy governing our environment. An understanding of all the schools is important because of the need to understand which adjustment or school is needed for a particular situation.

Landform feng shui is the oldest school of feng shui. It is based on the positions of the mountains and the rivers and on the basic layout of the land. Climate, contour of the land, and shape of the plot are taken into consideration when constructing a dwelling. Some masters believe that if the Landform feng shui is good, the occupants will prosper. In Landform feng shui, homes ideally are faced to the south for sun exposure. This provides protection for the front door from the harsh north winds. Farmland is also coordinated to water for lush growth and protection from the wind. Location, location, location is the key to Landform feng shui.

The terms "facing and sitting" positions are very important when dealing with this school of thought. The facing position of the home or business is determined by the direction our house or business is facing as we look out our front door. The facing position is yang energy, or active energy, coming into the home or business space. The architectural front door is usually used for the alignment of the facing position. Sometimes the front door may enter the home from a different angle or hidden entrance from the actual architecture of the front of the house. This may cause problems in determining the actual facing position. If this is the case, the facing position may be determined by placing the facing position where it feels the most energy coming toward the house, as opposed to the energy coming to the front door.

The sitting position is then the direction directly in back of the facing position. If your home is facing south, then the sitting position is north.

The Form School has the celestial animals of Chinese mythology. In Landform feng shui, the green dragon (large mountains), symbolizing good fortune, sits on the left, or east side of a home and should be higher than the tiger mountains.

The white tiger (lower mountains) sits to the right, or west, side of the house. The right, or tiger, side of a home, should be low key or calm to avoid waking the sleeping tiger.

The red phoenix is located to the front, or south, of the home, in the form of a small hill or hump. This serves as a footrest to signify a life of happiness and ease.

The turtle or black tortoise is located to the back, or north, of the home. The turtle should be placed directly behind the home in the form of a row of hills or trees. This served originally as protection from the north wind and as support to the dwelling.

For more information on Landform feng shui, I recommend any teachings or readings by Peter Leung, my master teacher. His teachings are some of the easiest to understand.

Compass School Feng Shui

The Compass School is based on the ancient *Book of Changes* called the *I Ching*. A Luo Pan compass is used for the compass method of feng shui. However, a regular compass will work, as long as you are acquainted with the I Ching or the Luo Pan method of feng shui. The Compass School method uses the compass directions in combination with a complex formula for determining the changing forces of feng shui within one's birth chart, which is called the four-pillar destiny. The four-pillar destiny is used to determine personal auspicious and inauspicious directions based on your time of birth.

The Compass School houses several different concepts of feng shui. These include eight mansion, flying stars, four pillar, and more. The flying stars annual chart changes each year in relationship to your natal chart and house chart.

The Lo-Shu square is used to determine the position that the annual stars fly each year (see The Story of the Lo-Shu Square, page 73). This information is used to help determine the most auspicious location and direction for your front door, stove, bed, back door, etc., for a specific year. The flying stars change yearly, monthly, daily, and hourly. It is important to understand how the movements of the flying stars interact with your personal natal chart. It is imperative to update your chart each year to capture the auspicious energy that is available and to negate the bad energy.

Black Hat Sect of Tibetan Tantric Buddhism

The Black Hat Sect School, or the Black Hat Sect of Tibetan Tantric Buddhism, is a school based on the teachings of Grand Master Professor Lin Yun. It is associated with "the intuition of the heart." This school of feng shui is the easiest to master and function in from a layman's point of view.

This is the school in which the body, mind, and spirit are developed. The body is used as the compass to feel the Earth's energies. The psychic or intuitive ability of the mind is developed to create a knowing. The spiritual is developed to connect the physical body to the Tao.

The Black Hat School is a mixture of Chinese culture and medicine, and Taoism, Buddhism, and Confucianism philosophy. In the West, Black Hat feng shui is considered an ecoscience dealing with chi (energy) flow, which promotes healthy living for the mind, body, and spirit. Black Hat feng shui is a combination of the use of mundane interior design and transcendental methods that use your intuition to create change.

Environmental consciousness and symbolism are also an important part of the Black Hat Sect feng shui. In Black Hat feng shui, intuition or psychic ability is used to obtain spiritual guidance and to create intention to obtain the adjustments needed. This information is obtained through meditation, which is based on the Tao. You are the connection between Heaven and Earth.

Mental alchemy is a term I like to associate with the Black Hat Sect School. Mystery schools for centuries have studied the ancient art of turning thought into materialized reality. The definitions of alchemy, according to *Merriam-Webster* (retrieved May 12, 2009, from http://www.merriam-webster.com/dictionary/alchemy), are as follows:

1) a medieval chemical science and speculative philosophy aiming to achieve the transmutation of the base metals into gold, the discovery of a universal cure for disease, and the discovery of a means of indefinitely prolonging life

2) a power or process of transforming something common into something special

3) an inexplicable or mysterious transmuting

In the Black Hat School of feng shui, that is exactly what we are trying to accomplish. We are using a process of transforming you and your home into something precious, either through physical manipulation or mental and spiritual awareness.

Alchemy, the forerunner of chemistry, is believed to have its origins during the first century A.D. in Alexandria, Egypt, where the arts of metallurgy and dyeing were practiced. The early alchemists were trying to change cheap metals into something more valuable. They also searched for the magic elixir of life to ward off death. Self-transformation was the goal of the most spiritual alchemist. A number of the earliest alchemical manuscripts were primarily concerned with spiritual and mystical properties.

Some of the earliest texts on alchemy are dated to AD 140 and were tied to Taoism, a philosophy and religion in China. These text were primarily concerned with immortality and prolonging life.

One of the earliest Chinese alchemists was Wei Po-Yang, who lived in the second century. Other mystery schools in Egypt, Greece, Persia, and Tibet were also studying philosophy and transmutation of physical and mental alchemy. The Great White Brotherhood, meaning "from the light," in Tibet practiced the belief that students on one plane of consciousness receive information from a higher plane of consciousness or "divine wisdom." Some masters of old, who are believed to be members of the mystery schools, include Jesus, Buddha, Amenhotep of Egypt, and Aristotle.

When Aristotle's student Alexander the Great conquered Egypt about 332 BC, the merging of Greek and Egyptian studies resulted in the prescientific study of chemistry called alchemy. Strides were beginning to take place in the finding of the "philosopher's stone," which was the element needed to transform lead into gold. The elixir to prolong life was studied in depth; thus, iatrochemistry was founded—medical chemistry. The power of prayer and meditation was a key feature in accessing this information from the "source" or the "higher power."

The alchemist knew the Spirit was always the driving force behind every project. It was the power that breathed life or chi through their bodies. As we begin understanding our spirit, much like the alchemists understood their spirits, we too can begin to create our reality through thought–mental alchemy. We begin to transmute thought into physical reality.

As we look at life in the twenty-first century, we have turned lead into gold, and we have prolonged life—internally and externally—with medicines, vitamins, and cosmetic surgery. Our potential is only limited by our thoughts and ourselves. Internal feng shui serves to make us aware of our thoughts and what we are creating for ourselves. We can then choose to change it for the better or stabilize it to become our reality, our goals, and our life. The time is now to use these powers of creation wisely and create realities worthy of who and what we are, not what we believe ourselves to be. Feng shui allows us to move this energy in our homes and in our bodies, minds, and spirits in a goal-oriented way to attain those goals.

The Black Hat School of feng shui and its applications of awareness teach how to do this on a physical, mental, and spiritual level. Transmuting thought into reality is a powerful tool to be used by the pure of heart, people who live according to the divine law, practice divine consciousness, and have only the best interest of humankind in heart. With feng shui, as in many of the alchemical works, the mystical and practical threads are so closely woven together that it is impossible to separate them. For many, the mystical is still alive, and the transmutation process is still a mystery.

Although all schools can function independently, an integration of the schools can definitely bring different dynamics and dimensions to a space.

In Conclusion

Feng Shui and Why It Works

As you know, feng shui is Mandarin Chinese for "wind and water." Because the language is very simple, interpreted it means energy, chi, or life force. Your life force.

Because of my feng shui studies, I became interested in more than the usual applications of feng shui. I have dropped into depths of the mind, body, and environment that I never thought were possible. In short, I have validated the fact that "I am my own feng shui."

Our environment has a huge impact on our behavior. It affects our lives whether we are aware of it or not. We attract, by the law of attraction, what we are putting out through our energy in our talk, our clothes, our home, our car, etc. To change this energy and attract those things we want, we must change our thoughts as well as our environment. Sometimes, however, bad things are just destined to happen to good people, and feng shui helps us to understand how to withstand the effects. Feng shui is not a cure-all for creating happiness but a way of living to help achieve a peaceful thought pattern and home, no matter what curve balls are thrown at us. Feng shui is a lifestyle and not a fad.

Four-Pillar Profile Analyses

Inner Feng Shui
Eastern Astrology

"Fate is never completely settled."

—Chinese Proverb

The four-pillar profiles and their analysis are complicated and a book unto themselves, but I would like to briefly touch upon it. The purpose of the four-pillar analysis is to help you understand the elements of the universe under which you were born and how they interact with your environment. The four-pillar chart is based upon your date of birth, your time of birth, and your place of birth. This interaction of elements can predict your destiny. The four-pillars chart enables you to understand the trends in your life and allows you to understand and create choices and courses of action.

Eastern astrology accepts as truth that when a body is born onto this Earth, it becomes in perfect harmony with the Earth environment at the exact second it was exposed to the elements of that day and time by absorbing those elements of the moment in the body. The combination of those elements are then carried with you throughout your life. This body chemistry, like your birthday, can never be changed. It is your destiny. However, the thing you can adjust is the environment in which you reside.

The calculations of the four-pillar analysis can help pinpoint the exact amounts of the elements (water, wood, fire, earth, and metal) born within the body. A perfect balance of 20 percent for each of these elements may be ideal; however, the likelihood of that happening is slim to none. It becomes extremely important to balance the out-of-balance elements with other factors within your body or your environment throughout your life. You can do this through color, food, clothing, furnishings, and people. This is why one may thrive better in the heat vs. the cold or why one prefers the color red to the color blue. This is also why we prefer one type of person to another. Your elemental balance becomes your energy field or force field inherently looking for survival and balance among the elements. The four-pillar profile may also be called inner feng shui. It is imperative before feng shui is added to your environment to research and comprehend what your own personal body makeup elements are because an over- or underbalance in the elements can cause stress upon the mind, body, and spirit.

Eastern astrology charts are similar to the Western astrology readings but are different in the calculations to achieve the readings. Do not confuse the two. However, the Eastern charts and the Western charts can be compared and researched further to help you understand your behaviors.

Each profile chart contains four pillars and a Ming Gua. Each pillar has a purpose and effect upon our life and destiny.

The Ming Gua element is the element of purpose and how you respond to pressure as an adult. It is the fate and destiny that will help you develop these skills. For example, Michael Jordan, a talented athlete, developed basketball skills, and Bill Gates, an intellectual, developed computer and business skills. Each element holds a piece of the puzzle to our fortune.

The hour pillar is your inner self and emotions, that part which is private to you. This pillar houses our spirit and intuition, which guide us through our senses. It is also indicative of career. It can be your creativity, or it can give you information about your children. This pillar can also reflect life in the golden years, in relationship to the day pillar. Note that if the profile does not have the exact time of birth, the day pillar may be inaccurate. All aspects of information are needed for an accurate chart.

The day pillar is the master self or body of self. This pillar is the key to all relationships in respect to the overall chart. This pillar helps determine your physical energy and stamina in your relationship to self, marriage, and spouse.

The month pillar holds our parental influences, tribal history, and DNA programming and imprinting. It helps you understand what supported you in your development. It is the headquarters of the four pillars. This pillar can be likened to the conscious mind. The month pillar shows the ability to transform in the other pillars. This pillar helps you understand why you respond to pressure the way you do, and it explains your interaction with your parents and siblings.

The year pillar is the outer self and how you appear to others through your personality and responses. This is what we are attracted to outwardly such as career, car, house, spouse, etc. The year pillar fluctuates with the year of the animal calendar. This could also indicate your soul journey or soul purpose in life in relationship to your daymaster.

The luck pillars of the four pillars are a ten-year cycle that fluctuates with the year of the animal calendar as well.

The energy of all the pillars relates to the day pillar and is analyzed based upon the percentage of their energy and yin and yang content, according to the generation cycle, degeneration cycle, and control and balance cycle found on pages 49 to 51.

The generation cycle is the cycle that supports or transforms into the next element. For example, *water* grows *wood*, *wood* helps *fire* to burn, *fire* burns down into *earth*, *earth* houses *metal*, and *metal* will make *water* as it condenses beneath the earth. Each cycle is needed to build the next. When a cycle is removed or an element compromised, all elements are weakened and the degeneration cycle occurs.

Be sure to be aware of the degeneration cycle in your environment. As one element supports the next, such as metal supporting water, the element supporting that element may become exhausted, much like if you were pregnant and nourishing another soul. It becomes extremely important to balance the interaction of these elements, otherwise this tends to be a destructive cycle.

Think for a minute about a wood and fire element mix. What does a little wood do to fire versus what a lot of wood does to fire? Too much wood can smother the fire, but a larger fire can also burn a little wood more quickly into ash. This is the yin and yang balance of the element cycle.

Say, for instance, we have a wood-based person working or living with a fire-based person who has too much of a fire element. If there is too much fire and too little wood, it will tend to exhaust or burn out a wood-based person, and illness may prevail. However, to remedy this interaction, we can put water in the environment to make the wood wet, and the fire energy will dissipate a little as it has to work harder to burn the wood. In this sense, the water has helped the wood control an overwhelming fire situation—which was burning up the wood element—thus making the environment livable and balanced for all.

Another cycle to be aware of is the control or balancing cycle. Think of a water and fire combination. Water can completely put out a fire, but fire can also boil the water and make it evaporate. So again, proportional measures are needed to preserve the balance of both elements. Too much fire or too little water can be adjusted with more water. Too much water and too little fire can be balanced with wood and more fire. Both draw energy from water. I cannot stress enough the importance of learning about the balance and combinations before hurling yourself into what could be disastrous feng shui.

With the element interaction in mind, this is how our environment can have an effect on the human body. Always be aware of the elements in the environment and how they interact with your body. There are also gods and deities associated with each interaction of the elements, giving even more insight into luck, career, marriage, and life's patterns.

Also, pay attention to the Chinese animal in your chart. Each profile has four different animals, and each animal has a different aspect for the year as it applies to family, health, emotions, and money. Layering the four-pillar charts can be complicated but well worth the knowledge you'll gain.

The historical calculations of the four pillars can be found in an original *Chinese Ten Thousand Year Calendar*. However, the book I recommend is an English version by Dr. Edgar Sung called *Ten Thousand Years Book: The Essential Tool for Chinese Astrology*. Profiles are available on various software, but be careful of these calculations because some are not always accurate. To receive an accurate reading, I would recommend using a qualified professional because mistakes made can be costly. Ask for credentials.

Ming Gua Numbers and Their Relationship to Your Destiny

The Ming Gua number is a fate and destiny number decided at birth; it cannot be changed. It is one of the areas of influence in our lives. It dictates two important qualities about us: who we were as a child and how we respond to pressure as an adult. It is our innermost spiritual quality as well as our spontaneity.

This number originates from the Lo-Shu square associated with Compass School of feng shui. It determines whether a person is an east group or west group. The east group is found in the directions of east, southeast, north, and south. The west group is found in the directions of west, southwest, northwest, and northeast. Use these directions to orient the front of your home, your desk or workspace, your bed, your meditation positions, and the dining room table.

The element associated with the Ming Gua can be used to strengthen and empower an individual. To find your Ming Gua number, start with your birthday. Add the last two numbers of your birth year together. For example, for 1968, add 6 + 8 = 14. If the answer is two digits, add those digits together one more time until you come up with a single digit (1 + 4 = 5). If you are a woman, then add 5 to this number; subtract 10 if you are a man. For a woman, you now have 5 + 5 = 10. Because the answer is two-digit, 10, add 1 + 0 = 1. The result is 1 for a woman or 5 - 10 = 5 for a man (don't worry about negative numbers). Your Ming Gua if you are a woman is 1 and 5 if you are a man (note: number 5 reverts to a 2). The number five is associated with the center of the ba gua, so if your Ming Gua is 5, change the number 5 to an 8 (woman) or a 2 (man).

Feng shui tip: You may strengthen your personal chi by using the appropriate color of your Ming Gua number or its generator element in the appropriate sector of the ba gua. You may also wear clothing of this color when you feel energy dragging.

The Ming Gua energy must be compared to the percentage energy of that element found in the four-pillar profile. Adequate adjustment to the element may be needed to reach your highest potential.

Ming Gua Chart and Its Components

Ming Gua Number	Color	Auspicious Directions
1 Career/Life Path	Water (black, dark blue)	East Group
2 Intimacy/Self- Love	Earth (yellow, orange, brown, pink)	West Group
3 Family/History	Wood (green)	East Group
4 Abundance/Wealth	Wood (green, purple)	East Group
5 Earth	Since all revolves around the 5 in the ba gua, the number 5 reverts to 2 if you are a man and 8 if you are a woman.	
6 Benefactors/Helpful People/Travel	Metal (white, gray, silver)	West Group
7 Creativity/Ideas/Children	Metal (white, gray, metallic colors)	West Group
8 Knowledge/Wisdom	Earth (yellow, orange, brown, pink)	West Group
9 Fame/Reputation	Fire (red)	East Group

Find your corresponding number in the next chart for your best directions and an explanation of why. For example, #1 Career corresponds with East Group #1.

Eight Mansions East/West Group

Based on your Ming Gua number, the following applications and directions apply:

Sheng Chi: Source of chi, best direction, good for all aspects of life

Tien Yi: Health direction

Nien Yen: Family, harmony, relationships

Fu Wei: Wisdom, growth, career

Ho Hai: Mishaps

Wu Kwei: Five ghosts, disharmony, lawsuits, small instabilities

Lui Sha: Six killings, unfortunate, divorce, failure, death, best position for bathroom to press down this energy

Cheug Ming: Total loss, accident, death, illness, bankruptcy, serious misfortune.

For professions corresponding to your Ming Gua element, read the sector on the elements, beginning on page 47.

Ming Gua Best Directions East Group

Ming Gua Number	Sheng Chi: Best Source of Chi, Good for All Aspects	Tien Yi: Health	Nien Yen: Family Harmony, Relationships	Fu Wei: Wisdom, Growth, Career
9 Li	East	Southeast	North	South
1 Kan	Southeast	East	South	North
4 Sun	North	South	East	Southeast
3 Chen	South	North	Southeast	East

Worst Directions East Group

Ming Gua Number	Ho Hai: Mishaps	Wu Kwei: Disharmony, Lawsuits, Instability	Lui Sha: Six Killings, Unfortunate, Divorce, Failure, Death, Best Position for Bathroom to Press Down This Energy	Chueh Ming: Total Loss, Major Loss, Accidents, Death, Illness, Bankruptcy, etc.
9 Li	Northeast	Southwest	West	Northwest
1 Kan	West	Northwest	Northeast	Southwest
4 Sun	Northwest	West	Southwest	Northeast
3 Chen	Southwest	Northeast	Northwest	West

Best Direction West Group

Ming Gua Number	Sheng Chi: Best Source of Chi, Good for All Aspects	Tien Yi: Health	Nien Yen: Family Harmony, Relationships	Fu Wei: Wisdom, Growth, Career
2 Kun	Northeast	West	Northwest	Southwest
6 Chien	West	Northeast	Southwest	Northwest
7 Tui	Northwest	Southwest	Northeast	West
8 Ken	Southwest	Northwest	West	Northeast

The 5 is also a west group. This number reverts to an 8 if you are a woman and a 2 if you are a man.

Worst Directions West Group

Ming Gua Number	Ho Hai: Mishaps	Wu Kwei: Disharmony, Lawsuits, Instability	Lui Sha: Six Killings, Unfortunate, Divorce, Failure, Death, Best Position for Bathroom to Press Down This Energy	Chueh Ming: Total Loss, Major Loss, Accidents, Death, Illness, Bankruptcy, etc.
2 Kun	East	South	Southeast	North
6 Chien	Southeast	North	East	South
7 Tui	North	Southeast	South	East
8 Ken	South	East	North	Southeast

Five-Element Theory of Feng Shui

Study of Element Interaction and Balance

Before going any further, it is important to understand the interaction of the five elements of the Earth and how they interact between living things and their environment. The interaction of these elements is important in understanding how to apply correctly the feng shui adjustments within all the schools of feng shui. The element interaction also affects our chakras which, in turn, affect our psychic or intuitive abilities.

All schools of feng shui consider as true the five elements responsible for the makeup of everything in the universe, including the human body. Each element has specific properties associated with a certain direction, body function, personality trait, and ba gua sector. When the Earth was created, the elements of water, wood, fire, earth, and metal came into existence. Everything on Earth from that moment forward sprang forth from these elements. Wind is air, and air is needed to sustain life. In feng shui, air is considered wood because the trees sway and circulate the air.

Each of these elements, as in nature, should be present throughout the home to create the feeling of balance and harmony. These elements play an important part of each ba gua sector of the home and are used to activate or control each sector, depending upon the circumstances in which it is to be applied (see ba gua map on page 78 for elements associated with each sector). Ideally, a balance of twenty percent of each element in the home or sector is desired to achieve stability.

If a sector of the home is feeling blah or lacking in energy, use the element associated with this sector or a support element to activate the energy chi of this sector. For example, if you want to increase the activity in the abundance sector of the home, use wood or water to lift the energy because the abundance sector is associated with the wood element.

If the energy in a sector is too swift or too abundant and we need to slow it down, use a degeneration element or a control element to slow this energy. For instance if a person's family is too demanding, then you may wish to slow some of that wood energy of the family sector with a little bit of earth. Balance is the key—not too much, not too little.

In nature, these elements establish a cycle in which they interact with each other to produce the perfect harmony of nature. This is called the tai chi. The tai chi is the never-ending cycle of life. We need morning to precede night and night to precede morning. Without night, there would be no morning. Without the sun, there would be no moon. Without the heavens, there would be no Earth. Without water, there would be no wood. Without wood, there would be no fire. Without fire, there would be no earth. Without earth, there would be no metal. Without metal, there would be no water. And without water, there would be no wood. This is the tai chi cycle that is needed to sustain life.

This is why the ecologists and environmentalists get upset over the destruction of the rain forests and undergrowth. The balance of nature is disrupted. This disruption may be the cause of the increased natural disasters. The tsunami of 2004 and the hurricane in New Orleans are good examples of bad Landform feng shui due to the destruction of vegetation along the shorelines.

The natural cycles of nature are the generation cycle, the degeneration cycle, and the control or balance cycle. See the chart on the next page to understand better how these elements interact with each other.

Interaction of Elements

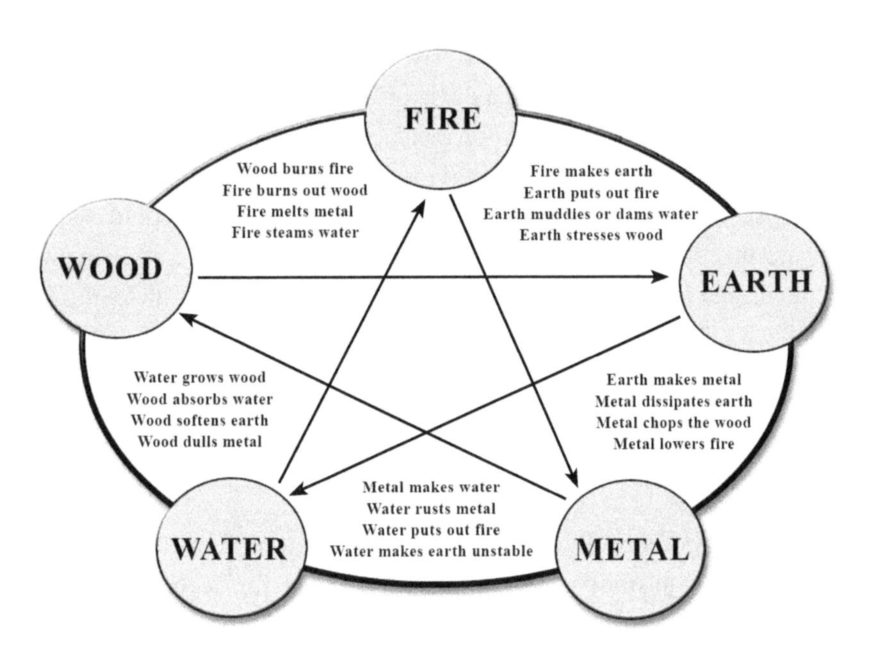

The generation cycle moves in a clockwise motion. Water nourishes, grows, and outputs wood. Wood burns and outputs fire. Fire makes and outputs earth. Earth produces, houses, and outputs metal. Metal nourishes, condenses, or outputs water. The output cycle in the chart becomes your ability to complete a project or process.

The degeneration cycle moves in a counterclockwise motion. Wood absorbs water. Water rusts metal. Metal uses up earth. Earth puts out fire. Fire burns out wood. This cycle can drain your energy.

The control or balance cycle moves across the board in a back-and-forth motion. Water puts out fire, but fire steams or evaporates water. Fire softens metal, and metal can balance fire energy. Metal chops wood, but wood dulls metal. Wood breaks up and roots out earth, but hard earth can kill a small tree. Earth muddies or dams up water, and water can cause the earth to become unstable. This cycle controls our luck and wealth.

We look at the chart to see what we control for wealth luck and what is controlling us for wealth drain. However, because it requires energy, this cycle can be exhausting.

Each element has a unique feature unto itself. Everything on this Earth is made up of one of the elements of the Earth, including you. Always remember that each design item must be completely analyzed before making a decision as to which element it belongs to, as it relates to feng shui principles. Plastic, for instance, is made from petroleum; therefore, it becomes the earth element. A mirror reminds us of water or ice; therefore, it is water. However, because it has the properties of silver in its makeup, it could also double as metal. Be aware that some of the design ideas can double for several elements. An element is first identified by its color, then its form or shape, and then its texture.

Water is just that: water or reflections of water. Metal usually means metal and electric products. Fire can be classified as lighting, warmth, and activity. Nature in all its splendor best describes the wood element. Wood is live plants, trees, flowers, fresh air, and wind. Wood elements must be alive and moving: green wood, not dead brown wood.

Furniture or dead wood is no longer in a state of growth and creativity but is instead an element in which rigor mortis has set in and is ready for decomposing. Therefore, a heavy brown wood armoire is first an earth element based on its color and its stocky form and is then a wood element based on its texture. A blue painted wood cabinet may be considered a combination of a water and a wood element.

Fire and water are the two catalyst elements that change shape and can move quickly or slowly, depending on the presence of the other elements. Chi energy is believed to build, gather, and move wherever there is fire and water.

There are foods associated with each element as well. You may use the food as an adjunct to help increase or support the element needed within the body, or you may use the food to decrease or control elemental effects upon the body. For instance, you may be a fire element person who is feeling “fired up” or stressed out; perhaps you have too much extra heat in the body. You may need to add more water foods to your diet to cool the body and control the heat. On the other hand, maybe you are a water element person with too much water energy in the body; then, of course, you would supplement your diet with fire food to warm the body. Each element, when combined with other elements, may become diluted or accentuated. The elements build upon other elements and must be assessed properly to get an accurate reading.

This book is only a general guideline to the elemental personality traits. The study of these charts and concepts takes years of practice. Reading this book and the profiles contained in it will not make you a professional. Get appropriate training and certifications.

Element Profiles and Their Relationships to Our Environment

Water

The oceans, lakes, and rivers of the world are God's perfect example of water. Water is the one element with a force that can destroy cities, continents, and cultures. As one falls into the belly or the abyss of the vortex of water, it can become the "bringer" of death. Tsunamis, floods, hurricanes, turbulent currents, and drowning are some of its manifestations. However, water can also be the "bringer" of life, such as the water of the womb. Water represents the cycle of life and death. It is from the womb that all life emerges and the mystery of the abyss to which we return. Water is used in baptisms, ritual bathing, and atonement or sacraments. In death, water is exhausted from the body. The body is 90 percent water and, nearing death, the body slowly dehydrates to prepare for the death process.

Water can flow around all obstacles that stand in its way. Water relaxes and restores our energy, whether it be in the body or the home. It releases and cleanses pent-up energy as it soothes and recharges the "qi" or life force energy. Adding water to an environment will help to activate wealth and abundance as well as the health (qi) energy. Any flowing water can symbolize creative opportunities coming to you or through your door.

Outside water should be placed to the left of the door as you are looking out the door. This is the dragon, or active, area of the home. Never place water to the right of the door. Outside, water should always flow toward the home but should not be rushing at the front door. Inside, water should be to the right of the door as you are looking inside. Inside water should never be pointed toward the front door or windows. Point it to the center of the home. Water should always be clean and unencumbered. Never keep a broken fountain or water feature in the home. Always get broken or leaky pipes fixed. This is symbolic of money, literally, going down the drain.

Water is a yin element. It is one of the catalyst elements because it perpetuates movement. Water is used to help move energy and release what is no longer needed. It may be still, meandering, or swift in nature. Water is movement and communication. Water creates wood and breaks down fire. Earth controls or balances water. Water is associated with the nighttime, preferably midnight. Its strength is found in the winter, and its weakest point is the spring when all the wood is in rebirth. The moon phase of water is the new moon. Water is associated with the direction of north.

Water is the element of mystery. It houses dreaming and thinking—it is the conceiver. It searches for truth and understanding of life. Be the water; go with the flow.

Water is associated with the kidneys and bladder, bones, lower back, and knees.

It is associated with the sense of hearing and the ears. The colors associated with water are black, indigo, or dark blues.

A water-type personality will usually be round and plump looking, but not necessarily fat. The water person has lots of curves, no matter his or her size. Water people's physical constitution may be weaker than other element counterparts, and their skin may tend to have a pale or bluish tint. They are usually physically cold, always seeking warmth from a fire or the sun. They may appear aloof and stuck-up, without the need to interact with others. They prefer solitude or one-on-one social interaction as opposed to large gatherings. They may have only a few friends with whom they fully connect. A water personality is very independent and prefers to work alone. Solitude is a must for a water personality. Be aware that water has many unpredictable qualities, as does a person with a lot of water in his or her charts. Do not underestimate such a person. Water people seem to have unlimited resources they draw upon. They are good at problem solving and research. They look under the surface and see the depths of a project. Water people, because of their resonant makeup, tend to be more psychic than the other elements, with the exception of fire.

Water people, when in balance, are calm, wise, solitary, philosophical, mystical, and deep and can usually "go with the flow." They have an inner strength and unshakable faith. The water personality has a vivid imagination and loves to tell stories. They dream and create easily. The water person, if in balance, loves to be around water.

An out-of-balance water personality is so emotional (too much water), dramatic, stubborn, anxious, unforgiving, phobic, manic, suspicious, and lonely that he or she may experience hopelessness and lack self-confidence. To the extremes, water people who are out of balance may be more prone to addictions and depression as well. They may also feel fatigued and weak. They may be sneaky and have a tendency to fib. The emotion associated with water is fear. Use earth or wood to absorb too much water, and use metal to support water. Water is used to control fire. Fire is the wealth element for water.

Careers associated with water are metaphysical professions, spiritual or philosophical work, or anything associated with research. Water people are usually comfortable, but respectful, around the water. Fishermen, boat captains, boat crew members, or anything dealing with water will intrigue a water profile Ming Gua.

Salty foods are associated with water. Because salt disrupts the water of the body, it is wise to eat salty foods when water is at full activity, such as in the winter. Get rid of the table salt and replace it with sea salt, available at all grocery stores next to the table salt. Water food is considered anything that cools the body. Use cooling food when heat is at the highest—summer. Any foods that are dark in coloration, blackberries, blueberries, eggplant, mussels, black sesame seeds, black beans, etc., are considered water foods, as are seaweed, shellfish, and fish. All things that are by nature salty and foods in liquid forms like soups are considered water foods. Also included are foods in their primal (egg or seed-like) form. This includes nuts and seeds. There is much crossover between foods, so you might want to pick what you are trying to achieve when designating the elemental makeup of a food. Most foods are more than one element, depending on what you are wishing to accomplish with the food.

The sector of the ba gua associated with water is the north sector of journey or career. On the esoteric plan of thinking, the journey can represent our path through life and all of its joys and sadness. On a mundane level, the career simply means what we choose to do with our life to make a living.

Design ideas to enhance water energy in the home or business are fountains, aquariums, fish, turtles, frogs, ships, vases of fresh flowers, vases of still water, seashells, pictures of water, ships, or seashores. Running water is used to increase your prosperity within the home. Fish symbolize abundance (eight gold and one black).

Aquariums or fish bowls are used to increase our luck and money protection. Ships symbolize our ship coming in and should always be hung so the ship is sailing into the home instead of out of the home. Bowls of sea water or rock salt may be set around the home to absorb negativity and calm unstable earth energy. A line of sea salt may be placed at your threshold to stop all negative influences from entering. Sweep it away periodically, and replace it with a fresh line.

Wood

Trees, plants, grass, flowers, fresh air, and wind are the part of God's world that make up the wood element. Born from water, wood is responsible for growth, expansion, and creativity in our lives. Wood elements are alive and moving, absorbing toxins from the air and sending back oxygen in its place.

Wood is symbolic of evolution. The wood's life cycle begins in the spring when the trees and flowers start to bud and bloom. The summer finds the trees in full bloom and at their peak of fullness and beauty. Then comes the fall when the tree starts to pull its energy inward as it begins its preparation for winter. The leaves begin to dry up as the tree pulls its energy to the trunk. By the time winter arrives, the tree's energy is completely drawn inward to sleep and conserve until it is time again to begin the cycle of life. Wood exhibits perfectly the life cycle of all living things. Each season has a time of beauty and a reason for being.

Wood symbolizes growth upward into the heavens. This upward energy is man's connection to the heavens, as the roots of the tree connect us to the Earth.

Wood is associated with childlike behavior. It is quick-moving energy, full of ideas, exploration, and creativity. When creativity is low, the psyche becomes low. Wood is needed when creating a new project or beginning a new undertaking.

A wood personality is usually tall and thin or muscular. They may be intense, driven, competitive, nervous, impatient, ambitious, and optimistic. The wood element is usually able to perform several tasks at once. I like to call this an ADD (attention deficit disorder) element because it is hard to hold a wood personality's attention for very long. They talk fast, think fast, and move quickly. They thrive on risk and adventure. You must learn to keep up with a wood type.

Careers for the wood personality are those that require creating new ideas such as advertising, media marketing, sales, travel, or working with people. Wood personalities love the freedom and flexibility to create. They need freedom in a job and the right to express their opinion. They do work well with others; however, their high energy may be off-putting or overwhelming.

It may be wise for the wood personality to work several part-time jobs and independent projects. They usually cannot tolerate someone watching over their every move. A wood personality has a need to work in his or her own time frame and not punch a time clock. This 9–5 confinement may cause the wood personality to become testy, angry, or frustrated, which may eventually lead to health issues such as migraines or eye problems. The wood personality, when out of balance, is prone to depression, and fatigue can easily set in. It is important that the wood personality find a balance between work and pleasure.

Wood minds are the minds of the pioneer and the adventurer. They love a challenge. They like to start the projects; however, once the challenge is met or the chase is over, they often lose interest before the project is completed. They have already moved on, mentally, to a new project, leaving the old one incomplete and stuck. Wood personalities need to recognize this tendency and pass off the project to a metal or earth person for completion before disaster sets in.

Unfortunately, the same applies to relationships. Wood personalities like to be entertained and excited, so the wood's partner will need to be as equally high energy or boredom will take its toll. Typically, the wood person loves to travel and see new horizons.

Wood creates and outputs fire and breaks down earth. Earth may also be used to stabilize or ground the wood energy. Earth becomes the luck element for wood. If wood energy becomes too exhausted, feed it water to revive and support. To lift the passion of wood, use a small fire. Metal is used for balance and control of the wood element. Use metal to help offset some of the high wood energy.

Wood is associated with the direction of the east, the southeast, and the morning chi. Wood is at its strongest in the spring and weakest in the fall. The moon phase of wood is the waxing moon.

The emotion associated with the wood energy is anger. Wood is associated with liver, gall bladder, and sinews such as ligaments, tendons, and skeletal muscles. It also controls the nails. Wood is associated with the sense of sight and the eyes. Clairvoyance is heightened in those with high wood content in their bodies.

The color green is associated with the wood element.

Sour foods are associated with wood. These foods act as astringents and benefit scattered, erratic persons. They tighten tissues and act as a diuretic for the body; think about sucking on a lemon or a pickle.

Food that grows on stalks or upward, such as corn, is associated with the wood element. Any green vegetable or herb is of wood value. Food such as chicken, liver, wheat, citrus, vinegar, pickles, lemons, olives, salad dressings, yogurt, and sourdough are examples of wood foods. Use these foods to detox and cleanse.

The ba gua sectors associated with wood are the family sector of the east, which holds the programming of the house and the people who reside there, and the abundance sector of the southeast, which holds the energy of wealth, health, and happiness.

Design ideas that enhance wood are trees, plants, blooms, flowers, or anything that projects upward, such as columns. Floral designs, tapestries, the color green, pictures of nature, and silk plants are acceptable as wood symbols. If you are not a gardener, dead plants are worse than silk ones.

Dried flowers are dead chi. They collect dust easily. It is not advisable to use these unless you intertwine them with silk greenery. One will offset the other. A word of caution: wood furniture falls into the earth category first because it is dead chi, and dead chi reverts to the earth. Wicker furniture can be classified as wood because of its airy, light feeling.

Fire

Fire, like water, is one of the catalyst element needed to transform energy as it awakens passion in our souls. The sun is the largest source of fire in the Earth's atmosphere. The natural sunlight is needed to help our body maintain its natural rhythms. It helps to lift the psyche, which is needed for those who suffer from seasonal affective disorder (SAD).

In ancient cultures, fire was considered the power of the Gods, the wizardry, and the mystery. The sun has been worshiped by cultures around the world for thousands of years. Each culture had a name for the ball of fire in the sky that appeared and disappeared daily. The Romans called their sun god Apollo while Helios was the name for the Greek sun god. The Egyptians called the sun Horus or Ra.

Fire has been used in purifications for centuries. Homes and household items have been burned to stop the spread of disease. Fire was used as punishment for those who did not conform to public demands. Witches were burned at the stake to stop the so-called "evil spirits." Legends say the Hawaiian volcano goddess Pele destroyed villages with molten lava when displeased.

Fire is the offspring or the creation of wood and is the most yang element in the universe. It is used for the expansion and the transformation of energy. Fire, like water, can be both dangerous and a vital part of the life and death cycle. Similar to water, it can be used for renewal, much like a forest fire burning away all of the old underbrush and trees, exposing new life and growth. Fire can burn lightly or so intensely that it consumes us.

Fire ignites our being and is the spark of passion for our desires. Spirit and passion can be seen in our eyes. Inner fire is our spirit, transforming and expanding every day in the body and mind. It is the internal light that guides us. As you light your own "violet flame" of consciousness in your third eye, you are able to project the future by listening to your inner voice. You gain access to the cosmic god, higher self, or universal power and become—in your own right—divine.

Fire celebrates what we wish to become. Without desire, we have no challenges or goals. Our fire passion continues to grow and change throughout our lifetime. Balance is the key to achieving our desires.

When fire or desire gets out of control or unrealistic, water is needed for balance. When desire is low, wood is needed to spark the fire. When we feel good, our passion is being fed. The emotion associated with fire is joy and happiness.

As the body prepares for death, the spark in the eyes becomes dimmer until extinguished when the body makes the transition from the Earth plane to the heavenly plane.

Fire personalities can be spotted by their fiery passion for life. They love being the center of attention. They are usually passionate, funny, flighty, and playful. They make a gracious host and have a flare for flirtation. They make sure everyone around them is having a good time. They love people and the party starts when they arrive. They are charismatic and have no trouble finding suitors. They need intimacy and security. They fear loss, dullness, and limitations. Their curiosity is contagious, but they hate surprises and confusion.

Because of their resonant makeup, fire personalities can be very empathic, and a career in metaphysics may fulfill their passion. However, the fire personalities love the limelight and would make great public speakers, actors, teachers, salespeople, lawyers, cruise directors, show business personalities, or any profession where they are the boss. They stir up enthusiasm and are team players and love the excitement of fanfare. If one has too much fire that burns too hot in his or her chart, he or she may wish to look at a water profession.

It is greatly important for fire people to love and be passionate about what they do, or else the passion of fire energy may die, and depression may result. Like the water element, in extreme cases, they can be prone to addictions or depression.

Fire persons will typically have a red hue to their hair and skin and will flush easily. They also suffer higher incidences of rashes and skin allergies because of this aspect. Fire is associated with the sense of feel and the heart and small intestine.

Fire energy is associated with noon—the midday hour. Its associated direction is the south. Fire is at its strongest point in summer and at its weakest in winter. The moon phase of fire is the full moon. The colors associated with fire are red and purple and also red-oranges.

Fire energy outputs earth and softens metal. Water is an essential element of balance for a distressed fire energy. Metal is the luck element to fire. Look to metal to reestablish boundaries that have been confused with anxiety to find perspective again. Use wood to help support an exhausted fire person.

Foods to support fire are bitter in taste. These bitter foods feed off water as cooling agents for the fire element. Bitter foods are lettuce, dandelions, citrus, artichokes, avocados, broccoli, peppers, cayenne, wine, coffee, and tea. These foods can dehydrate by reducing fluids and heat. These foods most benefit aggressive, overweight, or strung-out people.

The ba gua sector associated with fire is the fame sector located in the south. Fame may encompass reputation and notoriety in life achievements.

Design ideas to enhance the fire element first and foremost are warmth and lighting. Fireplaces, candles, incense, lighting, living things such as animals and children, pyramids, and anything angular in shape are minor fire elements.

Earth

Womb of Our Being—Peacemaker, Earth Supports and Nourishes.

The earth element is the mother of our life. It provides us a place to live. Earth energy provides grounding, and a sense of safety and security, and it supports and nurtures the physical being. It provides nourishment for the life beings on this planet. The energy of earth is more internal-womb-like. Earth creates metal and breaks down water. Wood controls or balances earth. Earth is associated with the afternoon, when things are settling in for the day. Earth is representative of all seasons. Its strengths are found in the last month of each season. The earth element's strongest season is linked to the Indian summer because of the maturity of the harvests at this time. The moon phase of the earth element is immediately after the full moon. Earth is associated with the direction of the center of the ba gua, northeast, and southwest.

The earth element is linked to the center of the ba gua—called the tai chi—better known as the health sector. The colors associated with the earth element are yellow, gold, brown, tan, and pink.

The earth element is associated with the abdominal area: the stomach, spleen, and pancreas. The sense of taste is linked to the earth. The sense of taste connects us to past desires, to what we have a taste for. Taste is closely associated with smell. Both evoke past memories. If memories are positive, taste is clear and desires are strong. If memories are clouded or negative, taste is voided. Overeating may become a problem. The emotion linked to the earth personality is worry.

An earth type personality is usually square and stocky. They may tend to carry weight around their middle. They tend to walk and move very slowly. They will talk hesitantly or slowly. Stuttering may also be visible in a strong earth personality.

Earth people do well in positions of command where they can help people: doctors, firefighters, psychologists, teachers, etc. They also like to work with the earth in the fields of horticulture, farming, or gardening. They need a solid income to feel secure. Any 9–5 job of interest to their element combination would be beneficial.

The high earth personality occasionally will have no concept of time frames and is usually fashionably late. They have a strong need for security and can be nurturing and diplomatic. On the flip side, they may be bossy and controlling. Like Mother Buffoon from the Nutcracker Ballet, the earth personality likes to make sure everyone and everything is okay. They are usually very easygoing, but they like things done their way. They tend to hate change or disruption. Get the wood personality to start a project, but use the steadfast earth personality to finish it. They will get the task done—just in their time frame.

An out-of-balance earth personality can be very stubborn. They often become very stuck in a behavior or rut and have a tendency to stay in relationships or jobs that no longer serve them. They tend to be pack rats and accumulate collections.

When the earth energy feels stuck, use water to soften the earth element. This allows the earth to shift and move easily. Wood and metal can also be used to break up the hardness of the earth exterior. When feeling insecure or unstable, the earth personality can use fire to restore and brighten energy.

Foods associated with the earth are carrots, potatoes, parsnips, radishes—any vegetable grown in the ground—plus apples, watermelon, beef, and fibers. These foods help cleanse toxins from the system and calm the spirits. Anything that involves sugar or fructose is also of earth association.

Ba gua sectors associated with the earth energy are the southwest of intimacy, the northeast of self-knowledge, and the health sector at the center of the ba gua.

Earth design ideas include anything massive in size, such as statues, rocks, or fountains that are used outside the home to anchor the corners of the home to balance the energy. Large furnishings, such as entertainment centers, overstuffed sofas, armoires, and trunks, are earth objects used inside as anchors in a home to stabilize fast-moving lifestyles. Other designs of the earth element include crystals and stones, terra cotta (both earth and fire), adobe, or stucco. Remember, items can serve two purposes or elements. For example, a dark navy sofa may be considered a water element with an earth element involved.

Metal

Communicate, Create, Concentrate, and Focus.

Metal controls the strong vibratory element of speech.

In the life cycle, metal is considered the old age or the dying cycle. The body starts with the water cycle, evolves through the wood, fire, and earth cycles, and ends with the metal cycle. The body, as it enters into the metal cycle, starts to dehydrate and grow stiffer. Physical energy gives way to mental or spiritual energy. The mind starts pursuing thoughts of God and afterlife, according to personal beliefs.

Throughout time, metal has been associated with wealth, money, treasure, and weapons. It is believed these things made one powerful. However, Chinese wisdom allows that knowledge or the inner workings of the mind are the real jewels or buried treasure of power. This understanding is interpreted as the "pearls of wisdom." Therefore, the mind, fed by metal influences, becomes the alchemist. The mental alchemist possesses the ability to manifest thought into physical reality.

The ancient alchemists, who attempted to turn simple metal into gold, became some of the first visionaries. They searched for the eternal fountain of youth. In this respect, metal has been associated with the patriarch of the family or tribe. The alchemist who keeps things in order and seeks out truth is inherent in each and every one of us who wishes to understand the mysteries of life. Knowledge is power.

Metal is the child of the earth. Metal is a yin element. It is very strong and focused. Metal outputs water and breaks down wood. Fire controls or balances metal. Metal is associated with the evening. Its strength is found in the autumn. Its weakest point is during the spring. The moon phase of metal is the waning moon. Metal is associated with the directions of the west and northwest.

Metal is associated with the lungs and large intestines. In the fall, it can be associated with the skin. The sense of smell is associated with the metal influences. Because the nose and lungs are so closely connected, any cold or flu may be affected by imbalances of metal in the body. The emotions linked to the metal personality are sadness and grief.

The colors associated with metal are white, silver, and rainbow or jewel tone—metallic colors.

A metal type is usually honorable and in authority or control, such as an employer or boss. A metal personality is disciplined and organized and appears businesslike at all times. They are intelligent and always in their heads. Somewhat of a control freak, they tend to be hard on themselves and others—a perfectionist. They respect authority and always adhere to strict standards. Their brain may work like a computer. They may tend to be aloof, analytical, proper, a stickler for the rules. They are methodical and predictable. They tend to see things as black and white; there are no gray influences. Military personnel usually exhibit a high metal content in their profiles.

In appearance, a metal person will usually walk stiff and upright. Some may be too busy to worry about appearances, while others are impeccable with not a hair out of place.

Metal charts sometimes are the hardest to understand because metal does not blend well with any element. If the metal person has lost control, become unsure of him-/herself, or reduced him-/herself to martyrdom, use wood to establish a sense of self-confidence and trust. Wood is the only element that can take the edge off the demanding metal chart.

An out-of-balance metal and water combination chart may be very cold, abrupt, and unreasonable. These people may seem self-righteous and judgmental. The chart may be sexually out of balance. Too much water is symbolic of sex, and metal is symbolic of desire. Use fire to heat and melt this cold frustrated influence.

A high metal and fire combination chart may be prone to abuse, cruelty, and volatility. Violence and danger may erupt from this combination. This type of combination may have a serious effect upon the lungs. Use water to dampen this tendency.

If there is a high metal and earth chart, the person may tend to get stuck in the mud and become lethargic. They may also be frustratingly stubborn. Use water and wood to soften the heavy earth tendency and allow the energy to move.

Careers associated with metal are military positions, management positions, or a career where they are in control. Research, electronics, computers, money or banking, and anything associated with mental challenges are great for a metal chart. They stay on task. They love to invent, calculate, and compute.

Spicy foods associated with metal are peppers, cayenne, ginger, curry, tofu, rice, onions, leeks, cinnamon, mint, spices, and fruits with thick peels, such as bananas. These foods help promote circulation or have a dispersing effect upon the body. These foods provide the most benefit to lethargic people who are cold all the time.

The ba gua sectors associated with metal are the benefactors sector of the northwest and the creativity sector of the west.

Design ideas to enhance the metal element are anything made of metal, such as wind chimes, metal furniture, llama bells, jewelry, or metal accessories. Items may include towel racks, candleholders, picture frames, computers, televisions, and electronic devices.

A word of caution: because we are in the age of technology, most homes and businesses are unbalanced in the metal element. Too much electromagnetic energy will drag and fatigue the aura of the body.

Yin and Yang Theory

The Tai Chi Symbolizing Heaven and Earth

Feng shui honors the yin and yang—the feminine and masculine in all things.

In addition to the elements of the Earth, feng shui also looks to the concept of yin and yang theory. The yin and yang theory is a way of seeing the world as it divides into two parts—a duality in all things. Each part of everything is dependent on the other for existence. One blends into the other, such as when the female needs the male to reproduce and survive, and the male needs the female to reproduce and survive. Day (sun) follows night (moon); night (moon) follows day (sun).

Yin symbolizes the Earth, representing Mother Earth and the feminine. It is the womb of existence. Yang symbolizes the sky, representing the heavens and the masculine. As Heaven and Earth are in place, so are mountains and the rivers. The weather of thunder and wind moves the energy with electricity and breath. Water and fire are in correspondence, not conflict. It is the nature of the cosmos. It is the Tao, working only with nature. This creates the tai chi, the never-ending circle of life. "As it is day now, it shall soon be night."

The white part of the tai chi circle symbolizes Heaven (yang) energy, and the black part of the circle symbolizes Earth (yin). The tai chi should be displayed with the larger part of the white at the top. This, in the I Ching, is known as Heaven over Earth, and it symbolizes the early Heaven arrangement in feng shui.

This symbol was mainly used for protection of the ancestral gravesites, as the Chinese believe the quality of the gravesites determines the destiny luck of the descendants. In today's feng shui, the Earth–Heaven arrangement is used for the feng shui outside the home or as a protection symbol for the home or business to ward off "poison arrows" from competitors who seek to do harm. The post-Heaven arrangement feng shui is used inside the home.

The yin and yang theory is extremely important in feng shui, as it balances the conflicts within an environment. The yang energy is more masculine in feel, and the environment may take on a more active or aggressive feel. If a space has too much yang, it may start to feel agitated and aggressive. It may also border on abusive behavior within the home or business because of the continual active energy. Every home needs downtime space, and that is why the yin energy is needed to balance.

Yin energy is a feminine energy and is more relaxed. However, if there is too much yin in a home or business, the energy may border on lazy, tired, and whiny. It may be too dramatic or emotional. This is why the yang energy is needed to balance and uplift the energy of the space.

Each room of your home is a yin space or yang space. The kitchen, the den areas, and the family rooms are considered yang energy. The bedrooms and relaxation areas of the home are yin areas.

The conflict begins when a yang room, perhaps a living room, needs to use yin space, such as a sofa bed doubling for a bedroom or a bedroom doubling as a workout space or office space. It is extremely important to make sure the balance is just right; otherwise, sleep will be compromised. Each space must maintain its own specific use, and that space should be used for that activity only.

Yin Qualities/Yang Qualities

Female/Feminine	Male/Masculine
Moon	Sun
Black	White
Cold	Hot
Soft/cozy	Hard
Dull	Shiny
Absorbent	Reflective
Thin	Thick
Nurturing/serious	Fun
Calm	Aggressive
Secluded, inactive, lazy	Busy, active
Water features	Fire feature
Sleep	Awake
Drapes, fabric, window treatments	Blinds or no window treatments
Overstuffed furniture, pillows	Straight line, upright backs, or hard furniture
Closed floor plan with walls	Open, expansive floor plan
Lots of furniture and objects/knickknacks	Less furniture and fewer objects/bare
Fringe, floral, or plain patterns	Geometric patterns
Things low on floor	Items placed above head
Clutter	Sterile
Tablecloths, doilies	Bare existence
Muted colors/pastels	Bright colors
Soft and flowing	Stiff
Textures: padded, rough	Smooth/plain

The information from the elements and the yin and yang theory is then applied to the actual living and working spaces.

Original Trigram Based on the Lo-Shu Square

The feng shui process first began with a mystical Chinese octagon, or ba gua, which contains the eight trigrams of life. This concept identifies eight different types of chi energy with a ninth energy in the middle symbolizing health, known as the tai chi.

These energies all build upon each other and circulate, clockwise, throughout the home. Called the Eight Aspirations of Life, each sector is associated with a number of the Lo-Shu square and an element of the universe. Everything in our life will fall into one of these areas. Each area has a yin and yang aspect.

The trigram, taken from the ancient book of the *I Ching*, consists of three parallel lines signifying different arrangements of yin and yang energies. Yin representing Heaven energy and yang representing Earth energy are the never-ending cycle of life.

The ba gua or eight-sided figure is considered to be a sign of good luck in the esoteric feng shui. This map can be applied in a pie form, shaped like the octagon, or it can be shaped in a square grid form. This ba gua is laid over the floor plan of your home or business. This map is representative of the energies within a home or business, and it tells a story of your home and your life's path.

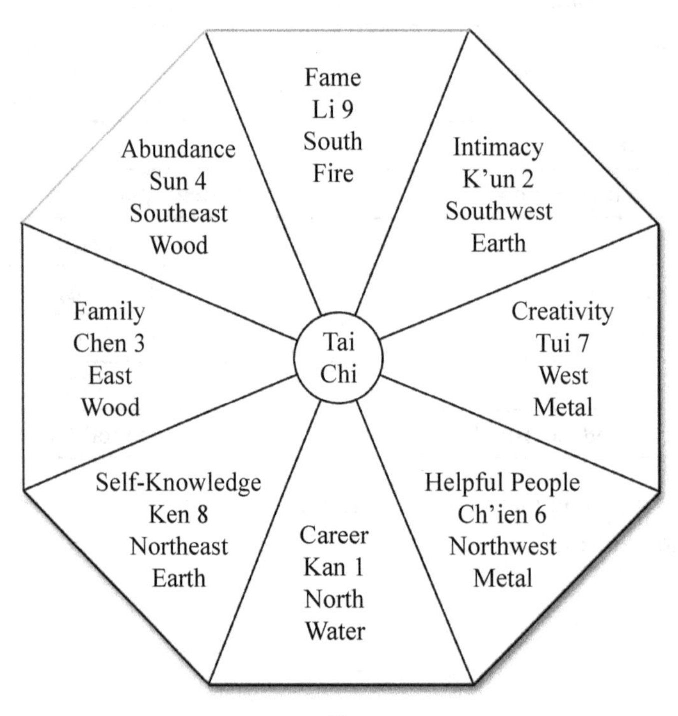

The Traditional Story of the Ba Gua

The story begins in the chen or family area of the ba gua. The chen (3) gua, on the middle left side or east side of the ba gua, is the beginning of the ba gua. It symbolizes the son of the king.

As we circle the ba gua in a clockwise movement, we go around to the sun (4) gua. This area symbolizes wealth, luck, and fortune. Next is the li (9) sector in the south, symbolizing reputation, friends, and higher self.

The intimacy gua or the k'un (2) is in the far right corner of the ba gua, the southwest, and it symbolizes the self. It symbolizes our relationships to others and our love and trust for ourselves as well as for others.

The next gua in this clockwise movement is the tui gua (7) or creativity sector. Located in the west, this sector holds the energy of children, conception, ideas, talk, and truth.

The subsequent gua in this journey is the chien or (6) helpful people sector. It holds the energy of teachers or mentors, guides and spiritual entities, and travel energy. This area may also carry the energy of war and of the people who helped out at that time—who, in the old time, were the ones who made the king powerful.

We now come to the middle of the bottom sector of the complete ba gua. This sector is the kan (1) or the win sector. This sector symbolizes the winning of the war or battles we face each day. We use these experiences to be king. The kan is symbolic of career or life path choices.

This brings us to the far left corner of the ba gua, which is the ken (8) gua. This is knowledge, which we accumulate from the past and present in order to live our lives in wisdom and peace and to prepare for our next journey.

The number in the sectors of the ba gua, in turn, corresponds with the feng shui number of the magic Lo-Shu square. Each factor of feng shui and its history build off another legend.

The Story of the Lo-Shu Square

Pre-Heaven/Early Heaven Arrangement

Shaman/King Fu Xi (4000 BC) is known for the beginning use of the Chinese metaphysical or divination arts. Usually portrayed wearing animal skins and surrounded by animals, he was known for his way with the animal. One day he saw a horse covered with a pattern of spots on his back emerging from the He River. This pattern of spots is known as the He Tu, the ideal order of the universe. These He Tu numbers are associated with the elements of the Earth and their interaction with each other and the Earth.

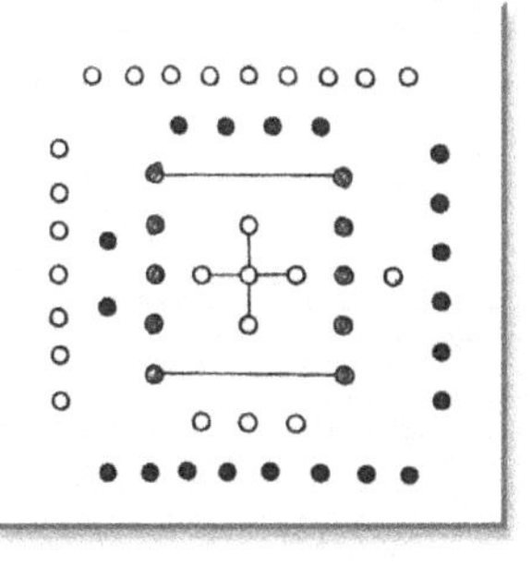

Enlarged Pre-Heaven Pattern

He Tu Numbers

The Ideal Order of the Universe

The He Tu numbers are elements which, in combination with other elements, blend into another, more powerful element, making a very auspicious combination.

Numbers Direction Blends to Make

1 (Water) 6 (Metal)	North	Water
2 (Earth) 7 (Metal)	South	Fire
3 (Wood) 8 (Earth)	East	Wood
4 (Wood) 9 (Fire)	West	Metal
5 (Earth) 10	Center	Earth

Post-Heaven/Late Heaven

Da Yu, a shaman (2300 BC), was an engineer who redirected and dredged the rivers to stop disastrous flooding of the lowlands. Legend says that one day he saw an enormous white tortoise emerging from the Luo River. On its shell was the pattern of the Lo-Shu square, which represents the current state of the universe.

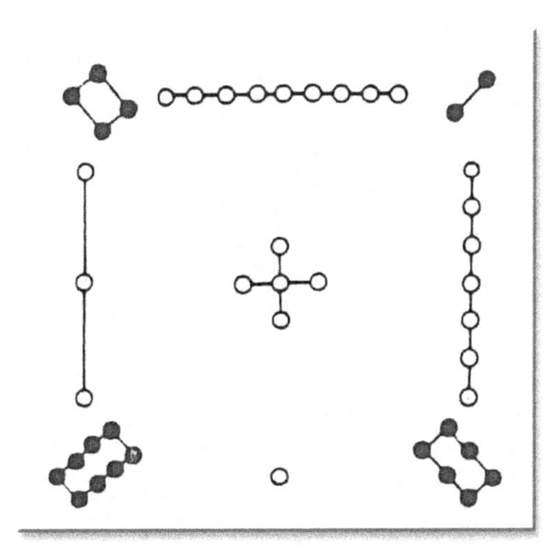

Enlarged pattern on the back of the tortoise.

The magic of the Lo-Shu square is that, when the numbers are added in a straight line or diagonally, they add up to the number 15. Hence, these numbers are associated with the post-Heaven ba gua.

4	9	2	= 15
3	5	7	= 15
8	1	6	= 15

The Magic Square or ba gua has been proclaimed.

The Current State of the Universe

Eight Life Aspirations of Ba Gua/Pa Kua Square

BA-GUA MAP

The ba-gua is a mystical Chinese Octagon, which has eight trigrams. This concept identifies eight different types of chi energy with a ninth energy in the middle symbolizing Health, known as the Tai Chi. Yin and Yang are in the middle of the Octagon. Yin representing Heaven and Yang representing Earth. This is the never-ending cycle of life.

This trigram has been westernized to fit into the Western Lifestyle of the rectangular or square home. The home should always be square or else certain energies of the home are not present. The map should be laid directly over a floor plan according to direction.

Ba-Gua Chart

<table>
<tr>
<td>Sun 4
Abundance Energy
(Wealth)-Southeast
Purple
Late Spring
Air, Wind, Wood, Water
Extremities, Liver, Gallbladder, Ligaments, Tendons, Muscles, Nails, Sight, and Eyes
Anger
Eldest Daughter
Solar Plexus 3rd Chakra</td>
<td>Li 9
External Recognition
(Fame) South
Red
Summer
Fire
Heart, Small Intestine, Blood, Head, Feel, Joy/Happiness
Middle Daughter
Third Eye 6th Chakra
Crown 7th Chakra</td>
<td>K'un 2
Intimacy–Commitment
Southwest
Silver, Pink
Late Summer
Small Earth
Spleen, Stomach, Pancreas
Taste
Worry
Mother
Spleen 2nd Chakra</td>
</tr>
<tr>
<td>CHEN 3
ANCESTORS
(History) East
Green
Spring
Wood
Extremities, Liver, Gallbladder, Ligaments, Tendons, Muscles, Nails, Sight, and Eyes
Anger
Elder Son
Spleen 2nd Chakra</td>
<td>TAI CHI 5
HEALTH
Brown/Yellow
Earth/Fire in the Belly
Heart /Spirit
Heart 4th Chakra</td>
<td>TUI 7
CREATIVITY
(Children, Ideas) West
White, Rainbow
Autumn
Metal
Lungs/Large Intestines/Skin
Smell
Sadness/Grief
Youngest Daughter
Throat 5th Chakra</td>
</tr>
<tr>
<td>KEN 8
SELF-KNOWLEDGE
(Wisdom) Northeast
Blue, Brown
Early Spring
Big Earth (Mountain)
Spleen, Stomach, Pancreas
Taste
Worry
Youngest Son
Root 1st Chakra</td>
<td>KAN 1
JOURNEY
(CAREER) North
Black/Dk Blue
Winter
Water
Kidneys, Bladder, Bones, Lower Back, Knees
Ears, Hearing
Fear
Middle Son
Root 1st Chakra</td>
<td>CH'IEN 6
HELPFUL PEOPLE
(Travel, Spirit, Community)
Northwest
Grey/Silver
Late Fall
Heaven/Metal
Lungs/Large Intestines/Skin
Smell
Sadness/Grief
Father
Throat 5th Chakra
Third Eye 6th Chakra</td>
</tr>
</table>

Line up your home according to directions—Compass Feng Shui

For the Black Hat School of feng shui, place the ba gua with the ken/kan/chien on the front door wall. For the Compass School of feng shui, line up the pa kua with the directions of the home and the land. The pa kua of the Compass School and the ba gua of the Black Hat are very similar and have the same qualities of aspirations within each kua or gua of the square.

Once you have identified the arrangement of your home with the square, a formula is used to identify your auspicious and inauspicious locations of the sectors of the home, based upon your time of birth. These areas of the home change each year according to your flying stars chart. The Compass School uses several methods to determine this: the east-west group formula, the pa kua lo-shu theory, and the flying stars theory. These methods are complicated and take many years to understand. If you are interested in having your eastern astrology charts done, I recommend hiring a trained Compass feng shui practitioner to insure accuracy of your charts. There are many aspects that factor into these charts.

The Flying Stars

Flying Stars feng shui can be difficult to understand. No aspect of feng shui is set in stone or follows a cookie-cutter style. The feng shui of a circumstance will change daily, based upon the energy of the flying stars.

Flying Stars feng shui, also be called Xuan Kong, meaning time and space, is the natal chart of a building, which describes its energetic condition over time. The Flying Stars method uses the sitting and facing directions of a building and its age as determined by the twenty-year cycle in which it was constructed. These number combinations reveal the energy of the nine sectors of the space. Flying stars charts include the original feng shui number, the period number, mountain and water star, annual star, monthly star, and their interaction with your ming gua number and four pillar chart. They can also break down into a daily star.

To obtain these numbers, it is important to know the year the home was built. The remodel history of a home is important as well, because the natal chart of the home may change if the house has been remodeled or recarpeted or if it has had a new roof or front door applied. That year, in turn, coordinates with a star number. (For example, a house built in 2009 coordinates with the number 8, which is the Wealth Star.) Find that number, and put that number in the center of the flying stars map.

Period 1—1864–1883

Period 2—1884–1903

Period 3—1904–1923

Period 4—1924–1943

Period 5—1944–1963

Period 6—1964–1983

Period 7—1984–2003

Period 8—2004–2023

Period 9—2024–2043

Period 1—2044–2063

With the period star in the center, a facing water star of money and finances lies at the front door, and the sitting mountain star of people lies to the back of the house. These water and mountain stars fly forward in a yang movement or backwards in a yin movement, depending on the properties of the stars involved.

Flying Stars feng shui can become confusing because of the details involved. The information associated with the flying stars is so extensive it could fill a book itself. Instead of reinventing the wheel, I would like to recommend that you buy a good Flying Stars book or take a class on Flying Stars. Lillian Too, Peter Leung, and Simon Brown are some of the easiest-understood authors on the subject of the flying stars.

If you wish to try a simpler method, I recommend you use the annual flying stars technique. This technique is easy and focuses on the aspects of the yearly flying stars, the sectors they fly into each year, and their effect on your life.

Annual stars change with the Chinese New Year. Each star has an inherent capacity and affects a part of your home and life each year. The strength and the properties of the annual stars are compared to the aspirations of the home and the element of that ba gua sector. Do a mini analysis on your home to see how the annual stars may affect that part of your life for the year. This takes practice, intuition, and paying attention to the patterns of the year and the years gone by.

Each year, the annual star center number decreases in numerical size. The annual stars are as follows:

For the Year 2009 Center Star—9

For the Year 2010 Center Star —8

For the Year 2011 Center Star —7

For the Year 2012 Center Star —6

For the Year 2013 Center Star —5

Stars continue in a descending order—4, 3, 2, 1 . . . back to 9.

Each number of the flying stars holds an aspect and energy strength. The annual numbers and their properties are as follows:

The #1 White Star of Luck is good for career, fame, and fortune. It is timely to the Period 8 energy and is of moderate strength. To activate this star, use the water element.

The #2 Black Star of Illness is inauspicious and can cause lawsuits, robberies, and accidents. It has a strong influence and is of the earth element. Use metal to weaken.

The #3 Jade Star of Conflict is responsible for misunderstandings, conflicts, and robbery. When paired with good stars, it may become neutral. It is weak and of the wood element. Use small amounts of fire energy to weaken.

The #4 Star of Literary and Film Success is full of intelligence, recognition, and achievement. It is of the wood element and very auspicious. The #4 star is also considered the Peach Blossom Romance. Place 4 bamboo in water to enhance.

The #5 Yellow Star of Instability (Wu Wang) is the bad boy that causes hardships, misfortune, and disasters. It is especially inauspicious when paired with a 7, 2, or 9 star. One should never sleep or work in a yellow star area. It is a strong earth element but can be weakened with metal, water, and salt.

The #6 White Star of Fortune and Luck is good for authority and power. It is especially good when paired with other auspicious stars. It is of the metal element and can be enhanced by metal such as Chinese coins.

The #7 Red Star of Evil is competitive, confrontational, lawsuit-encouraging, and unstable. It is of the metal element and can be weakened by water energy.

The #8 White Star of Wealth is very strong and timely in Period 8. It is a very auspicious earth element. It is most powerful for money. Use citrine stones to strengthen.

The #9 Purple Star of Expansion or Celebration is a very strong fire energy and may be auspicious or inauspicious, depending upon the energy of the other stars around it. Use lighting to uplift the energy, and use water to downplay energy.

Place the annual number for the current year in the middle of the chart, and fly the stars according to the flight pattern. Below is the original Lo-Shu square and its flight pattern. Each year, with a new number in the center, these stars will have different effects on each sectors.

Eight Life Aspirations of Ba Gua/Pa Kua Square

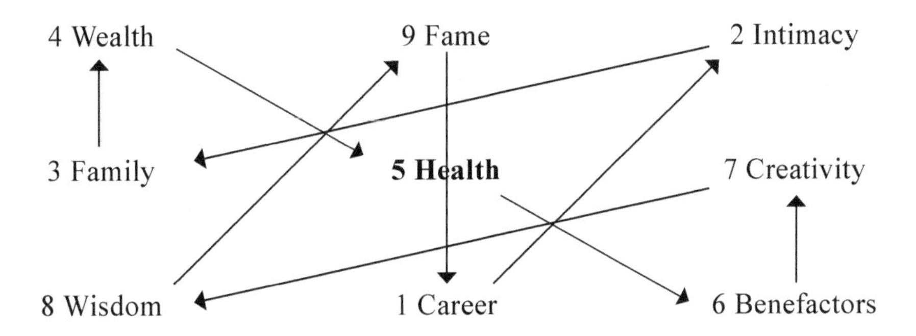

Starting at the health sector, follow the pattern from the center of the map and go to the benefactors of the northwest (6). Now go up to the west (7) and cross over to the northeast (8) and up to the south (9). Now go down to the north (1), up to the southwest (2), and cross over to the east (3), up to southeast (4), and back to center.

This flight pattern lines up in a sign of the Sigil of Zuan Kong, which resembles the Kaballah's Sigil of the planet Saturn. Sigils are considered to be part of "ancient secrets" in some cultures. The Zuan Kong Sigil holds within it the energy of the flying stars and its movement from year to year, period to period, and second to second. This Sigil with the triangle at the top and the bottom is believed to symbolize resurrection, completeness, and wholeness. In the Hebrew tradition, the Sigil is believed to be perfect, as it was visible in the sky the night Jesus was born.

Now compare where the annual stars line up with your ba gua and see how these energies will affect your life for the year. Layer this information with your four-pillar profiles, the layout of your home, and the natal chart of your home if you have it, to make an assessment of your home.

For example, the star combinations of 7, 2, 9, and 5 in the east or family area may cause illness, instability (lawsuits and robbery), and possible death to members of the family. A star combination of 4 and 8 in the west area or creativity area may mean money from writing or film. Look for all aspects of these combinations. Make the necessary adjustments to enhance or press down these areas. Read about the ba gua sectors in this book.

Other factors in Flying Stars feng shui that must be addressed are the Three Killings, or San Sha, and The Grand Duke, or the Tai Sui.

The planet Jupiter, which is a thousand times larger than Earth, appears to move in a direction opposite the sun; this opposition appears to have an effect upon the pull of the Earth. Each year, this pull positions itself within a different degree or direction of the Earth. This disturbance is called the Grand Duke, or the Tai Sui. This upheaval may bring loss and illness to this direction of the home. Do not dig or disturb this area of the home during this movement. Do not face this direction as you work or meditate. It is best to have the Grand Duke at your back for support. Use a Pi Yao or the animal sign corresponding to the direction to help release some of the Grand Duke energy.

The Three Killings is also a sharp energy that should not be disturbed. Fight off the energy of Three Killings with trees and flowing water. The trees will block the energy and the water pushes back the energy of the Three Killings. You may face the Three Killings but never sit or sleep with your back to it. The most important thing to remember about the Grand Duke and the Three Killings is to avoid disturbing the area until the influences have left.

Part THREE

Principles of Design and Feng Shui

The same principles of design that constitute a design theory or governing concept of a design and that make it work together successfully are fundamental in feng shui design. These principles are exceptionally important for a good design layout within the home to help the body and mind feel balanced.

Scale and proportions incorporate the size of a space, and objects in this space must be of the same scale or size. A huge space and tiny furniture or a small space with huge furniture is proportionally out of balance. The size of window treatments in relation to the size of the window or even the size of the back of a chair in relationship to the size of its arms can affect the equilibrium of the room. Always keep scale and proportions in balance.

Balance is the state of equilibrium that is achieved by arranging architectural details, furnishings, or patterns. They may be either symmetrical (exactly the same on each side of a center point), asymmetrical (different on each side), or radical (spokes or concentric circles). An out-of-balance room has an out-of-balance effect on the body.

Rhythm is the smooth flow (chi) of elements that carries the eye around the room. This may include repetition and alternation of patterns or an idea, or a transition of ideas.

The important thing is to make sure the room flows together so it does not feel blocked by an abrupt stoppage of movement, such as the design taking us to a blank wall. This will feel as though we have hit a dead end in the home.

Emphasis is the focal point of a room. It may be a fireplace, a piece of furniture or architecture, or a painting. A room may contain more than one focal point in varying degrees of dominance. Use rhythm and balance to combine the focal points. Not identifying the focal point can lead to a backward feeling within a room. All energy should flow to the focal point.

Harmony (variety and unity) is the selection of compatible elements and furnishings that create a pleasing whole, or in other words—feng shui.

Elements of Design and Feng Shui

These elements are the contents that form the principles of feng shui interior design. The elements are seen in the arrangement of architectural structure and details as well as in the compositions of materials, furnishings, and accessory items.

Space: Define the space—use open and closed areas and positive space versus negative space to create a flow of energy. The space needs to be balanced according to size and the number of furnishings for that space. Look at how the space will be productively and appropriately used according to feng shui principles.

Shape or form: Shapes must flow easily and rhythmically. Too many shapes confuse the eye and cloud the mind.

Mass: This is the actual or visual weight or density of a form. Remember that balance and proportion are key when working with mass.

Line: Line is the connection of two points that gives direction: vertical lines are the wood element, horizontal lines are the earth element, angular lines are the fire element, wavy lines are the water element, and curved or rounded lines are the metal element. Each elemental line has a psychological impact on the body. Is it soothing or jolting? Is it serving its purpose?

Texture: The texture is the relative smoothness (yang) or roughness (yin) of a surface. Texture is read physically by touch or visually. Very small patterns are often read as texture. Always ask, "What emotion or energy am I trying to evoke, awaken or capture?"

Pattern: The arrangement of motifs used to create a unified design is a pattern—for example, the pattern seen in an area rug or upholstery design. Always decorate within your energy range. Too much busyness in a pattern causes confusion and overburden.

Light: Natural sunlight and artificial light (lamps, bulbs) affect the appearance of all other elements of design. If possible, make sure to have natural sunlight during the daytime hours, and have it coming in at least two windows. Be careful of heavy window treatments, especially if you need extra light (fire energy) in your environment.

Color: Color carries a psychological impact. Be aware of how a color affects you. Colors can vary from light to dark and from intense to muted. Find the color that best works for you.

Color Theory

Color is a large part of our lives, and it affects our psyche every day. It should be used in abundance in our homes and on our bodies. The following chart expresses how different colors may affect your being.

Red: Fire energy—warm color, represents physical movement, sex, love, passion, anger, and pain. Aggressive color. Governs 1st chakra. Associated with the fame area and south of the ba gua.

Orange: Earth—warm color, represents self-empowerment, strength, success, joy. Governs 2nd and 3rd chakras. Associated with self-knowledge (northeast), health (center), and intimacy (southwest) areas of ba gua.

Yellow: Earth—clairvoyance, communication, cheerfulness, grounding. Associated with learning. Governs 3rd chakra. associated with self-knowledge (northeast), health (center), and intimacy (southwest) areas of ba gua.

Green: Wood—warmest of the cool colors represents healing, prosperity, nurturing, nature, calm, and stability, growth, and hope. Governs 4th chakra. Associated with family (east) and abundance (southeast) areas of ba gua.

Blue: Water—cool color. Invokes emotional and intellectual activity. Lighter shades of blue may produce tranquility. Used in meditation, as it can calm the body. Bright blues can stimulate thought. Dark blues and black can become depressive. Use in small quantity or with jewel tones. Governs the 5th chakra. Associated with career area and north of the ba gua.

Purple: Harmonizing color; contains value of warm (red) and cool colors (blue). Associated with the regal, spiritual, magical, and intuitive. Governs the 6th chakra. Associated with the abundance area of the southeast.

White: Purity, Protection, and God. Governs the 7th chakra.

Black: Absorbs negative energy. Combination of all colors. Use to help clear 1st chakra.

Gray: Neutral color; use to activate benefactors. Evokes no emotions. Too much of this tone lowers body energy. Be careful of this.

Brown: Grounding, security. Associated with the earth. Can be used for health. Use to help strengthen 1st, 2nd, and 3rd chakras.

Pink: Muted fire energy. Color of love, gentleness, femininity, and harmony. Governs 4th chakra. Use in intimacy area of the ba gua. Associated with 1st chakra, and can be associated with the 4th chakra.

Peach: Color of drama and flirtation. Do not use too much in the bedroom. Produces too much energy. Associated with 1st chakra.

Gold: Godly kingdom; associated with the 7th chakra.

Silver: Deep wisdom; the moon; woman. Associated with the 5th chakra.

Feng Shui Adjustments

Light-Refracting Objects

Mirrors are considered a feng shui cure-all, but be careful of too many in a home. Mirrors can speed up and redirect the flow of chi throughout a living space. If chi flows too quickly, it can do more harm than good. A mirror attracts positive energy or good chi into a living space. It opens and expands areas to help solve design problems. Mirrors give the illusion of a virtual space by providing reflection and adding energy to a room. When properly placed, they are symbolic of doubling wealth.

The feng shui function of a mirror is to "seal in" the negative force coming at the mirror and reflect it back to the source, thus protecting anything positioned behind the mirror. The mercury in the mirror is the metal responsible for sealing in the undesirable chi. Concave ba gua mirrors are used at the front door to deflect or absorb bad chi coming at the home or business. Mirrors project a watery quality as well as a metal quality.

Leaded-crystal, faceted balls are infused with symbolic power to activate chi and disperse threatening chi. Crystal balls reflect, expand, refract, and diffuse energy. Do not "crystal ball yourself to death." The size of a ball should be proportional to the size of the energy infraction. Use only leaded crystal, as it pulls the energy of the body upward.

Lights are considered the fire element. Lights can stimulate weak energy and move chi upward. Up lighting is great for dark corners and depressed chi. Where there are cobwebs, there is depressed chi. You will feel more energized in a brightly lit room. A dark room can be depressing. Fire and reflective surfaces also enhance lighting factors in a room.

Sound

Sound vibrates the air, lifting stagnant energy and redirecting fast-moving energy. This, in turn, helps the chi to resonate on one energy level, creating harmony within the body and home. Make sure the sounds are not too tinny and that they resonate with your body tuning. To reverberate energy, most practitioners use wind chimes, bells, tuning forks, and tuning bowls.

Anything with a melodic sound can also be used to move or vibrate the air or chi. You may use CD players, stereos, drums, pianos, and other musical instruments to move chi. Do not place wind chimes in the southwest or northeast sector of the home. It is yin energy and is believed to invite spirits into the home. Do not place wind chimes in the center of the home, except in circumstances where the energy in the entire home is depressed. Wind chimes in the center of the home may promote too much activity.

Living Things

Plants, flowers, and aquariums have nourishing chi and lift energy. Plants have a life force that makes a room relaxing, and they absorb toxins from the air and replace them with oxygen. Any pets or children are chi lifting.

Traditional Chinese Cure Objects

The traditional Chinese cures are the symbolic adjustments used to visually uplift our thoughts and symbolize what it is we want our home to represent. Bamboo flutes represent peace and harmony. Red firecrackers, three-legged frogs, turtles, fish, red envelopes, and coins represent wealth. Fu dogs, ki luns, pi yaos, Kuan Kung, coin swords, and magnetic hematite are used for protection of wealth. Rose quartz and mandarin ducks are used for love and harmony. Wu Lou gourds, metal calabashes, and magnetic hematite are used to guard health. Use Buddha, Kwan Yin, or Christian symbols of Christ to bring the spiritual aspect into your home.

Moving Objects

Negative ions create positive attitudes. Moving water pulls positive ions from the air and cleanses a space. Water recharges qi and adds vitality to the environment. Adding a fountain or aquarium to your home or office will activate wealth and health energy.

Nine goldfish (one black and eight gold) symbolize abundance. The black fish is believed to absorb negative energy. Aquariums also bring good fortune and money protection.

Prosperity is believed to be increased with moving water. Moving water also helps communication with others. Water fountains, hot tubs, streams, waterfalls, flowing bird baths, or mobiles generate positive chi and neutralize menacing chi.

Wind socks, weathervanes, windmills, flags, and/or anything moving stimulates chi. Moving objects hold the eye in perfect harmonic balance. These movements help create serenity of mind and help foster our thoughts and creativity.

Heavy Objects (Anchors)

Rocks and heavy statues can stabilize the energy of a place or a situation. Placed in the right spot, an unsteady relationship or career can improve. Heavy furniture and trunks also serve as anchors. You may place anchor objects in areas of the home that contain bad flying stars number combinations. This imprisons the power of the numbers and does not allow that chi to move as freely and cause added trouble. Remember to frequently move the objects and clear the energy around the objects and space.

Electrical Objects

Computers and televisions add energy to a room. Putting a computer in the "wealth" corner of your office can lead to greater business success. Always hang a crystal over a computer to disperse energy and help prevent fatigue. All electrical objects and appliances stimulate chi, but be careful of too much energy coming at you, which can cause exhaustion. If these objects seem to activate the area too much, unplug them when not in use. Use magnetic hematite or black tourmaline to dispel energy.

Colors

Artwork, painted walls, and decor colors can enhance and balance chi flow, create peacefulness, and encourage good fortune. Each color has a psychological effect on the body, mind, and spirit. Be sure to understand the effect each color has on your personal well-being to ensure peace and harmony within your living space.

Fragrances

Fragrances are such an important part of our lives. Smells, both good and bad, influence our journey through life and have a strong impact on how we respond to our environment. From the womb, programming of the sense of smell has a significant impact on the quality of life. Smells from our life become programmed into our subconscious mind and set triggers to our memories. This can instill a sense of security and protection or a sense of fear. The emotions of grief, sadness, and regret are linked to the sense of smell.

Fragrances and essential oils have been used to clear space and balance the energy of homes for centuries. Religious texts have touted the uses of essential oils in purification, healing, and embalming rituals. A pure therapeutic grade oil is preferred to a perfume grade because it has the highest frequency of any natural substances.

Every living thing has an electrical frequency. Measuring in megahertz, Bruce Tainio Technology in Cheney, Washington, developed equipment to measure the biofrequency of humans and foods. He found that a healthy body has a frequency measuring from 62–78 MHz. Disease begins to introduce itself to the body at 58 MHz. However, it was discovered that 100 percent therapeutic-grade essential oils still contained the "life force" of the plant, and measured from 52 MHz to 320 MHz. Clinical studies show that essential oils have the frequency and chemistry to help us maintain an optimal health frequency within our environment. Other studies show that processed food has a frequency of 0 MHz, and fresh produce and herbs varied from 2–27 MHz. These studies show that essential oils have double to triple the frequency of food and herbs.

During these studies, when oils were diffused into a room, clients felt better emotionally. Within seconds of their introduction, the clients became calmer and less anxious with their research environment. In controlled testing, it was found that minor unhealthy substances in food and in the environment lowered the body's MHz, and recovery time from a minor infraction took up to three days. It was also discovered that negative thoughts lowered the body frequency by 12 MHz, and meditation and prayer increased the measured frequency by 15MHz.

It is imperative to educate yourself on the use of these oils and keep your living space olfactorily correct. It is so important to become aware of what fragrances enhance your well-being. Essential oils, aromatherapy, incense, cooking and baking, or familiar smells will enhance the chi of a room. A musty room depresses chi.

Transcendental Remedies

These mystical symbols or rituals need to be applied by a qualified feng shui practitioner.

Rules for Feng Shui Enhancements

To set intentions and activate more powerful chi when applying a feng shui remedy, focus on your intent. For example, to improve your career, visualize how you see this intent taking place in your life—such as a job promotion. Anytime you make a feng shui adjustment, always reinforce using the three secrets. Your intentions can become very powerful, however, so be very careful what you wish for. Be very clear and precise on your creation of manifestation. Always follow this process using the three secret reinforcements.

Using the Three Secret Reinforcements:

The purpose of the three secret reinforcements is to anchor a physical object to a mental, physical, or emotional state. Create a clear intention and add "with harm to none" at the end of each intention.

To integrate the body, use a mudra or hand position that matches your intent. This anchors the shift in the physical body. This is the physical anchor.

To integrate the mind, use a visualization to create a mental reality for what you are working toward. This is the mental anchor.

To integrate the spirit, use a mantra or affirmation with the power of sound to anchor your spirit body. A popular Buddhist mantra used is Ohm Mah Ni Pad Meh Ung (pronounced "Ohm Ma Ne Pad Me Hum"). This means love, light, truth, peace, joy, and oneness. Say this mantra nine times. This is the spiritual anchor. Feng shui uses traditional Buddhist methods; however, use your own spiritual belief system for your spiritual anchor. Supply your own prayer, or the word *Ohm* if that fits your intention.

Adjustment for new energy or transforming energy should be used between the hours of 9:00 a.m. and 1:00 p.m., when the yang energy is at its strongest. To stabilize or balance an energy flow, use between the hours of 9:00 p.m. and 1:00 a.m. This is when the yin energy is at its peak. The twelve o'clock hour is always significant. Meditate before your intentions, and perform the intentions with a calm, peaceful mind. Many blessings to you.

Note: These cures are taken from Master Lin Yun videotape, *Creating Environments for Success and Well-Being.*

Tips for Effective Space Planning Using Interior Design Feng Shui

The following tips are important aspects to look for when applying feng shui to a home or business. Although the adjustments are too numerous to name, these tips give you a starting point. From these, layer other adjustments on them.

Always check out the chi of the land. Landform feng shui is the first and foremost consideration. Is the left, or dragon, side of the home—as you are standing in your doorway facing out—active? Is the right side inactive? Is the back of the home protected? Is the front of the home free from obstruction? Are there any sharp corners or poison arrows pointed at the home?

The chi passing over the land to get to your front door should be fresh and healthy. The grass or foliage should be lush and green. The birds should be singing and plentiful. The area should be well kept. What is the economic situation of the neighborhood?

Important exterior factors are the road directions. Is the traffic moving swiftly in front of the home? Is the home or business at a T intersection? Are there more than two streets intersecting in the front of the home? What is the position of the home within the cul-de-sac? Are there an excessive number of power or telephone lines or transformer towers within five hundred feet of the home? Is the foliage in the area struggling? If you answered yes to any of the above questions, my advice is keep on looking. These factors are very inauspicious for a home or business. You should always have full vision of the property. There should be no hidden corners to hold "dead" chi. Hidden corners, also known as hidden dangers, will also decrease security.

Always plan for the house and lot to be square or rectangular; otherwise, you may have some missing guas in your home. The shape of the lot and the shape of the home or business should be square or rectangular to avoid missing ba gua spaces. These areas, if missing, can affect the eight aspirations of the life journey. If you have a missing ba gua sector, you can complete the area with a courtyard, garden, deck, or patio. Use mirrors on the interior walls of the missing area to simulate the illusion of the wall extending outward into the missing area. The garden or courtyard actually will become a room of the home and needs to be treated accordingly.

Pay attention to the front door. Feng shui deals with the movement of energy through a home or business. This energy follows the Earth's movements and moves through the dwelling in a clockwise motion. Like the mouth is to the body, the front door is to the home. It represents the "mouth of chi." This is the place fresh, new chi enters and flows through the home. The toxins of the home, or used chi, exit out the back door. Make sure the paths to both doors are unobstructed. The path to the front door must always be unobstructed so opportunity can find you.

The placement of the front door and what it says are important factors when we enter the home. Is it a pleasant area, or is it congested? To allow new chi to flow into the home daily, use your front door every day. Many of us today use side doors and the garage door, so it is essential to open our front door daily and let new chi or new opportunity come in. You don't eat through your ear, so don't expect your home to get its fresh air source from the garage entrance and car fumes.

Social contact is very important in human life. The front door should also have an open line of communication to your neighborhood. A home's front door with a direct and unobstructed view of all the neighbors is more desired than a hidden doorway. Security is improved if the neighbors can see your front door. In apartment living, the front doors should meet at a common meeting area to encourage open communications with neighbors.

The Dalai Lama tells us we must meet our neighbors and get to know their families to make peace with and respect each other. If neighborhoods and apartments are constructed with the front doors in view of each other, we can't help but meet our neighbors and develop a rapport. The layout or the way our streets and houses are organized will affect the way we feel about ourselves and our neighbors.

Sometimes planning the layout of the home is impossible. Few homes are automatically feng shui correct. If floor planning is not an option, be sure to ba gua out each room, and activate the room according to the ba gua, based upon the room and the individual's needs. Each room of the home should have a specific use and should be used for that purpose only.

All major traffic paths through the home should be at least three feet or more wide—the wider, the better. Most objects project a three-foot aura field, making a narrow traffic path feel more constricted and congested. Dowsing rods may be used to confirm this. Minimal clearance for traffic within secondary pathways such as between two chairs, is eighteen inches; however, twenty-four inches is more desirable. Each chair needs three-feet of extension room for our legs. Three feet of clearance between bed and dresser is advantageous. Always be aware of the traffic flow in and out of room entrances. Keep all traffic areas open and clear.

Clear the clutter in the home. Clutter creates confusion and obstacles in our lives. It holds a vibration level that prevents chi from moving freely about the home. Clutter holds tired energy. Organize and clear out all items you have not used for the last year. Give them away or have a garage sale.

Move objects off the floor to lift the spirits. It is proven that depressed people look at the ground more than they look up. Objects, baskets, and clutter on the floor can obstruct movement of your feet, legs, and hips and prevent you from moving forward in life as quickly. Floor objects may also inhibit foot chi and cause foot, leg, or hip pain. To lift the spirits, hang pictures above eye level. You may also consider a border wallpaper at the ceiling to lift chi.

As you go through your home clutter clearing, make three piles: one to keep, one to toss, and one called the "maybe" pile. Find those things that you love and use regularly and keep them. Find those things that you hate and get rid of them. Find those things that you aren't sure whether you love or hate and put those in the "maybe" pile. Go through your "maybe" pile frequently and decide whether to keep or toss each item. I guarantee that after you take a couple of trips through the "maybe" pile, you will toss it all. You must love everything in your home. If it is broken and you don't fix it right away, get rid of it. It holds stale energy. This stagnant energy makes your home smell stale. Make sure your home always feels and smells fresh. This has a direct impact on the well-being of the body.

In ancient China, bathrooms were located outside the home in a communal area. Bathrooms are tough rooms to put in a ba gua because of the downward, flushing energy. A bathroom should never be located in the center of the home. When a toilet is flushed, it takes air from the room to push the water down the toilet. As it flushes, it literally flushes energy down the drain, much like the vortex of a tornado. This subsequently disturbs or creates a drag on the chi around our aura and energy center of the body. Because of the excessive water energy going down the drain, the metal element in the creativity area of the west is a good place to put the bathroom. It will support the lost energy going down the drain.

Always flush with the lid cover down to help avoid some of this problem. Keep the lid cover in the down position when not in use. Also, keep the sink and bathtub drain covers closed if you feel you are losing energy in your home. However, be aware that the air must circulate through the pipes to keep them working properly. To adjust this problem, hang crystals in the bathroom.

The bathroom is a good place to create thoughts. As we are readying ourselves for the day, we think a lot. We create our appearance, plan our day, and dispose and cleanse our bodies of all that is not needed anymore, thus clearing the path for newfound ideas. This is the place the psyche gets put together in the mornings. Old beliefs must be dumped before new behavior can occur. What better place than a bathroom?

Kitchen or dining areas do well placed in the family area of the east, abundance area of the southeast, or creativity area of the west. A kitchen should be arranged in a triangle, with cabinets between appliances. The stove is the fire element, the sink is a water element, and the refrigerator is the metal element. Never have the stove touching the other appliances in the kitchen. If they do, make sure there is a piece of wood or cabinet separating them.

The stove is the largest Fire element in the house. Esoterically, the stove symbolizes health, vitality, and wealth. The stove symbolizes the healthy food used to nourish the body. You should never see the stove or back door from the front door position. Stoves should never be located in the northwest corner of the house. A stove is a fire element in a metal sector and can be dangerous for the occupants, especially the father.

The stove should be situated so the cook can see the activity of the house. When his or her back is to the room, there is the tendency for the cook to feel vulnerable, and he or she may soon develop a tendency to dislike cooking. A mirror or piece of stainless steel strategically placed on the stove helps monitor activity behind the cook and may help to remedy this situation.

The stove should have plenty of headroom between it and the hood or fan. Too little headroom gives the impression our head is being cut off, and we have to duck down to see the stove. The stove must be in good working order. A dirty stove stagnates the flow of wealth and makes it harder to keep. Always rotate the use of all burners to make sure the energy flow is even. Attract extra money chi with healthy plants in the kitchen. Keep the kitchen light and airy; don't use dark, heavy colors.

Keep the counters and refrigerator free of clutter. Install appliance garages below your counters to hide everyday clutter.

This is actually a refrigerator. It is very bad feng shui with all the clutter. It can also lead to bad eating habits. Solution: Get a cork board and post the tidbits of information and pictures on it. Locate it in the creativity area, if possible.

All family members' bedrooms are best when located in an eastern location. This allows the morning sun to activate the hormone that activates the immune system. This is the only time of the day this particular chi level is activated. It is proven that eastern-location bedrooms have healthier occupants. Bedrooms should also be located in the back quadrant of the home to prevent road activity from disturbing sleep patterns. Guest rooms may be located elsewhere without concern.

No electrical equipment, electrical panels, or gas meters should be located outside a bedroom wall. The power will arc through the room causing EMF disturbances to the body. Children are especially sensitive to the electrical energy. Pay especially close attention to the feng shui of a child's room.

A bedroom is a yin space used for sleeping and intimacy. The bedroom should be a sanctuary for whoever is sleeping in that space. It should be luxurious, clean, organized, and a place to relax—no distractions.

A couple's bedroom should be for adults only. Children should not be sleeping with their parents full-time, as this destroys the intimacy of couples. There are always extenuating circumstances to every rule, but children must develop boundaries and respect for their parents' space as well as learn to develop a space for their independence.

No photographs of children or parents should be located in the couple's bedroom, either. This room should never contain dirty laundry, children's toys, big boy toys, computers, or treadmills. The bedroom is yin space for sleeping, and the treadmill or computer is too yang and may disturb rest. If you place a television in your bedroom, make sure it is at least eight feet from the bed.

The bed's headboard should be placed in one of your auspicious personal directions, according to your ming gua chart. If there is a conflict in a couple's chart, the head of the bed should be placed in the direction of the one who is struggling the most. This helps support their energy by energizing the conception vessel at the top of the head.

Always be aware of drafts floating over the bed. The bed should never be in a direct line to the door, nor should it be placed between a door and a window or under a window. If this placement is not possible, make sure to add heavy window treatments to insulate against the "King of Evil" draft.

A bed should not be positioned on a bathroom wall. The bathroom wall will produce too much water movement energy for restful sleep. It will drain energy from the occupants of the bed.

Do not place your bed in a direct line with the toilet. It becomes a sha chi or bad energy. Place a mirror between the toilet and the bed if this is unavoidable.

Do not locate ceiling fans above the bed, it disturbs the aura of the body as you sleep. A solid headboard is needed to protect the crown chakra on the top of the head or the conception vessel. Hang a crystal over the head of the bed to help open consciousness while sleeping.

Be sure to sleep on pure cotton sheets and in pure natural sleepwear. Sleeping in the nude is ideal, as it allows the body to breathe. The body has a freer range of motion, and its ability to rejuvenate and energize is increased. Try this for a couple of consecutive nights and see if it makes a difference in your sleep pattern.

A den or office will do well located in the abundance area of the southeast, the fame area of the south, the benefactors area of the northwest, or the self-knowledge of the northeast. An office should be used only as a place to do your work and not a place to view television; otherwise, you will not get much work completed, as the television will distract you.

Desks should always face the doorway, but not be in direct line with the doorway. This is the command position of the room. Do not place your desk facing a wall. It will feel as though you are always "hitting a dead end." If the desk faces a window, one will tend to daydream as they stare into nature. If a desk is in direct line with a doorway, this will cause the occupant to be distracted by the activity outside the room.

A desk should be large enough to accommodate the size of workload involved. The bigger the desk, the more important the person and work involved. An office chair should have a high back to protect you from attack. The higher the back, the more important and more protected a person will feel. Ba gua out the desk top, and activate its sectors according to the ba gua map.

The center of the home or health area ideally should always be open and free of walls, closets, or halls. If closets are located in this area, be sure they are clear and free of all clutter.

In the home, staircases should never be located in the middle of the home. This tends to allow chi to fluctuate and may cause fatigue and illness. If this occurs, hang a leaded crystal at the top of each staircase. This helps to disperse the chi and stabilize the home's energy.

Always pay attention to exposed beams, pillars, or posts in a room. Low ceilings with beams will tend to depress or cut into chi. Soften these obstructions with vines, bamboo flutes, or cloth. High ceilings are not as much a factor as low ceilings.

Pay attention to what your home is saying to you. Everything in your home has an effect on the body, mind, and spirit. We experience everything through our senses of sight, sound, touch, taste, hearing, plus the sixth sense: knowing. Make sure everything in your home is "senses correct." Be aware of what each item is symbolically saying to you.

If anything holds negative thoughts or feelings, get rid of it.

What does your artwork, knickknacks, or furniture say to you or about you? If you have to think about whether you like an object or not, chances are you do not, and you may as well let it go. Check out how each of these six senses "feel" in the home. Close your eyes and feel the energy around those senses. Make your environment happy and cheerful. Fall in love with your home again and everything in it. Make it your sanctuary.

Pay attention to how you respond to the colors in your environment. How do they make you feel? Are they too much or too little? Are they too monotone or too eclectic? Do not be afraid to experiment with color. Colors have a direct effect on the psychological and physical well-being of the body, mind, and spirit. (See the section on color theory for more information.)

Lighting is also important. Make sure to have great lighting in your home. Spectrum bulbs are the best. They are more expensive, but they last longer and produce a better light. Replace light bulbs as they burn out.

Make sure your home is always in top condition. Make repairs immediately. Do not let plumbing or water problems remain unfixed. A coat of fresh paint goes a long way, is affordable, and helps clear energy in a home.

Remember as you clean your home, there is a place for everything and everything has a place. Maintain the cleanliness of your home daily. Clean your house, especially your kitchen, before you go to bed at night, and make sure it welcomes you in the morning with a positive message. NEVER leave dirty dishes in a sink.

Keep your yard and trees trimmed. The trees and vines should not touch the home. This hinders the chi from circulating, plus gives the feeling that something keeps "scratching at you."

Clean your windows regularly. Dirty windows cloud the mind and distort the eye. Make sure all windows are in good condition.

Pay attention to the element balance of water, wood, fire, earth, and metal within the home. Also, balance out the yin and yang elements. This promotes harmony and balance, similar to that found in nature.

Your home is the blank canvas to painting your life. You are your home and your home is a reflection of you. What do you want that reflection to be? The condition of your home has a direct effect on the health of your mind, body, and spirit. It is one of the most expensive things you have . . . use it wisely.

Feng shui is an inexpensive way to recreate your home or office. This can be done by de-cluttering, remodeling, painting or by putting up mirrors, chimes, crystals, and water objects to help soothe, slow down, speed up, or deflect the flow of energy through your home. Do your research, pay attention, and see what changes are occurring as you make adjustments within the home.

Feng shui used in the commercial space can improve customer/employee/management relationships and increase productivity and profit margins.

REMEMBER: Always trust your intuition, no matter what someone else says. Your mind knows what is best for you. Listen to it.

Ba Gua Sectors, Symbology, Feng Shui

Adjustments Made Easy

Homes hold conscious and subconscious meanings. The following are recommendations to help bump the subconscious mind into a paradigm shift. Place these items in these directions or ba gua sector of your home, office, or individual rooms.

As you enter your home, the door is considered the mouth of chi, or the entry for the beginning of your journey in this home. The energy in your home corresponds to the energy coming from the direction it faces.

Each of us is in a specific home for a specific reason, and that purpose is shown to us as our life progresses. Our home or business is the universal consciousness that gives us our life experiences. You are anchored in place for a learning experience. The learning experience is why you may have chosen a rambler home versus a two-story home, or perhaps a home with a basement, or a home that faces a particular direction. Whatever the choice, there is a reason. Go deeper into your behaviors and find the answers. There are no mistakes. When the journey in a specific home is complete, there will be a desire to move or remodel. You will inherently feel that completion and need a fresh start.

From this moment forward, see your home as a living, breathing entity of yourself. Pay attention to the direction the front door of your home faces and the symbolism behind it. This gives purpose to your reason in this home.

Esoteric Journey through the Ba Gua

Journey (Career)—North/Kan

The ba gua begins in the north of water, symbolizing birth or our life journey and life path purpose. It becomes our mother. Meditate in this sector for answers to your life's purpose. This sector, on a mundane level, can also mean your actual career or business success. The journey sector is ruled by the number 1 of independence in the Lo-Shu square. Water is the energizer that helps manifest a higher self, and from this incredible state where everything is possible, individual consciousness is developed.

A north-facing home is considered a Kan facing/Li sitting home. Water energy outputs or creates wood energy. From the water comes creativity and growth. The north sector is associated with and fortunate for the middle son. The middle son or middle-aged man will find power in this sector and may wish to locate his office or bedroom here when the annual flying star is auspicious.

Water symbolizes money and wealth flowing to you. If your front door is in this area, place a fountain on the left side of the door as you are looking outside. The fountain should be placed so it is flowing toward the direction of the front door, but not directly in front of it.

Place objects of water or wealth in this area to increase career opportunities or money flow. A three-legged frog facing the front door or the abundance area of the southeast is desirable for money luck. The frog should be elevated off the floor, as this shows an order of importance. Vases of water or bamboo in this area are also acceptable.

Use ships, fish, turtles, seashells, or blue crystals also to activate the water energy of the north. These features should always be pointed toward the center of the home and not out the door or a window. For example, a picture of a ship sailing into the home may symbolize your "ship coming in." Be creative.

The water energy is also associated with sexual activity. To activate your sexuality, use curved shapes and wavy designs or flowing designs. The color black and an array of blues are also associated with the water energy.

Because water energy may hold emotions, be sure to place bowls of sea salt throughout the home to absorb and clear negativity.

If the energy of the north is too cold, unwelcoming, or out of balance, use fire energy in this area to offset cold water energy. If the front door faces the north, place fire energy as well as water energy at the front door. Lighting is an excellent activator for fire.

Self-Knowledge (Wisdom)—Northeast/Ken

From birth, the learning process begins. As you travel clockwise in the ba gua, from the journey sector of life path, you must learn wisdom. The northeast or the self-knowledge sector is your next stop in the ba gua. This sector of your home relates to belief systems, self-knowledge, learning, meditation, and studying. Use this area to learn more about yourself and others on the physical, emotional, and spiritual levels. This is a great area to facilitate change in your life. This area is good for meditation and soul searching. This is also a great space for the children to study. Learning is easier in this sector.

The self-knowledge area is controlled by big mountain, and metal or mental energy is the output energy. No water should be placed in this area, as it dilutes the energy of the mountain. The northeast is ruled by the number 8 or infinity ∞ in the original Lo-Shu square. Until the year 2023, this is a money sector for the Period 8 Flying Stars feng shui.

The northeast facing home is considered a Ken facing/Kun sitting home and is very auspicious during the Period 8 Flying Stars period. This sector is associated with and fortunate for the young man or youngest son. The youngest son will find power in this sector and may wish to locate his office or bedroom here when the annual flying star is auspicious.

Use this area to shift your paradigm of self and get in touch with who you truly are. Place objects in this area that you wish to manifest internally. This area houses the belief system of self and how you respond to it. If you are trying to lose weight and maintain a healthier lifestyle, always place objects in this space of positive progress.

In my home, my northeast sector had pictures of peasants slaving in the fields. They were famous prints of the paintings the *Gleaners* and *The Angelus* as well as the *Song of the Lark* and *The Harvest*. These images symbolize backbreaking work. The message given to me during childhood was, "You must work hard to get ahead." Because of hard work in my life and a lack of a support system, I had developed a lower back problem, compounded by a back surgery. Once I noticed the message in my belief system sector, I immediately removed the pictures from that sector. Be careful of all items and messages in this sector.

Place items that can be used to enhance your life into this sector. Place items here that you would like to believe in. If you wish to believe more in yourself, place items of strength and courage. Use dolphins to access your higher self.

Place books and a private chair in this area to study or meditate. However, make sure you keep your study books on one shelf and your pleasure books on another. Each subject has a different energy attached to it. Bookshelves should be covered or kept tidy at all times. Placing yellow crystals or rocks in this location will help you connect with your inner consciousness.

Because this is the original 8 or money sector of the ba gua, it may be used for money enhancement as well. For money enhancement, citrine stones, yellow crystals, or items totaling 8 can be used in this area. Minimal water should be used in this area. Because this is Period 8 of the Flying Stars feng shui cycle, this sector is very strong for money for the next nineteen years. Use it wisely.

Use the colors of yellow, orange, brown, and other earthy colors in this area; also use small metals.

Ancestors (Family)—East/Chen

The cycle of life continues through the ba gua, clockwise, from the birth of north, to the prospects of learning in northeast, to the discovery of family and its roots in the east of the home. The east represents all that has come before us. This sector houses the history of our ancestry. It encompasses the history of our ancestral family tree, DNA imprinting, family dreams, beliefs, social status, and actual immediate and extended family members.

The east is ruled by thunder and big wood (trees). Its output is fire or passion. The east is represented by the number 3 in the Lo-Shu square. The east home is a Chen facing/ Tui sitting home. The eastern sector is associated with and fortunate for the elder son. The elder son or older man will find power in this sector and may wish to locate his office or bedroom here when the annual flying star is auspicious.

This gua sector provides the stability for the family and teaches us the need to branch out from family on our individual life paths. Loyalty and nurturing are qualities of this gua. The family sector is considered the house of the rising sun and new opportunities. Its focus is growth and creativity.

The east also holds the history of the home. The history of the land and home are very important because, like the people who reside there, it has been imprinted as well with history. Find out the history of the ground the home sits on. Was the ground a past burial ground? Was the ground a cow pasture? What was it? Go to the city office building in the zoning department and ask.

Next, research the history of the house. If the house has been through a bankruptcy, fire, death, suicide, divorce, or any other trauma, this energy has been imprinted in the walls, floors, and ceiling and will affect those who reside there.

To clear the energy, open all the windows and doors and spray this area with a blend of about ten drops of orange essential oil and about five drops of frankincense essential oil in a twelve ounce bottle of water. Adjust according to smell. Be sure to spray all door and window frames. You may also ring a chime to help move and resonate energy.

For the outside of the house, hire an outside shaman, priest, or qualified spiritual person to come bless the ground with a prayer ceremony.

Family issues will gather in this sector. Spray the home weekly to dissipate any past, present, or future negative health, financial, or relationship issues that may arise within a family unit. If a family member is ill, increase the light in this area to promote good health. This sector of the house should be cleared with orange oil on a weekly basis.

Place current pictures of family members and loved ones in this area. Take down all pictures of couples who have been divorced or partners who are deceased. These pictures will hold sad memories for the family. Be careful of the display of too many deceased family members. You do not want a shrine in your "living" home.

If a family member has become estranged or is far away from the family, such as in the military, place a picture of that person with the family in the east. Make sure the picture was taken at a time of happiness, such as vacation, and not at a funeral. Place a light and a spiritual deity, such as Buddha or Jesus, by it, and this will help that person find his or her way home. You may even place a prayer for safe return.

Items in this area can set the pace of a happy, changing family or continue a chain of long-time unhappiness within a family circle. This is the area to break any chains of unrest or abuse. If there are problems or chains of behavior to be broken, place a deity in this sector with a picture of the person who needs help and offer a prayer asking for help, gratitude, and forgiveness. This technique may also be used in the intimacy area of the southwest.

Place heirlooms or antiques of family here. Again, make sure these are items of happiness and not those that hold the energy of illness, abuse, or unhappiness.

Use live or silk plants, especially fig or pine trees, in this area for longevity. Decorate with the color of greens and warm spring colors, or use green crystals to lift energy. Use purple to harmonize this area. Place fresh flowers or floral patterns in this area to support the wood energy.

Negative energy or quarreling can be controlled with a little bit of red in this area. Be careful of a red front door in the east. The excessive fire energy may bring fire hazards or family conflict.

Abundance (Wealth)—Southeast/Sun

From the discovery of family, one has grown and is now moved to start accumulating and developing a self outside of family. The next step in life is the accumulation of wealth, health, and happiness.

The southeast or Abundance sector is ruled by air/wind/wood/water, representing movement and new growth. This sector represents all those things that make our life richer. The southeast may also represent literary or film acknowledgment. The southeast home is a sun facing/chien sitting home. The southeast sector is associated with and fortunate for the eldest daughter. The eldest daughter or older woman will find power in this sector and may locate her office or bedroom here when the annual flying star is auspicious.

This area can be used to help you trust that the universe does provide you with whatever it is you need at any point in time. As you open yourself to the abundance the universe has to offer, you will discover that abundance just keeps flowing into your life—just look for the signs.

The Abundance of the southeast is used to increase abundance of wealth, health, and happiness. It is considered the fortune corner. You will become abundant in anything you place in this area, so be selective and willing to do the work attached to it. I wish to caution you: be careful what you wish for.

For money luck, place actual money, if possible, in this corner. You may use the traditional feng shui cure of nine Chinese coins tied with a red string, symbolizing wealth, in this sector. You may also place nine Chinese coins under your front door mat to welcome prosperity into your home. Put coins and paper money into piggy banks.

Place money frogs, plants, money, and red envelopes, bamboo, or green or purple crystals in this area for money luck.

Place plants or bamboo in this area. Rubber plants or jade plants are symbolic of money shapes. Flowering trees and fruit trees are great. Add elements representing small water. Do not use too much water, or you will wash away your abundance.

This sector is the original number 4 of the ba gua, which symbolizes relationship. Place relationship or partnership pictures in this sector. A small running water feature may be placed here, as long as it is not in the bedroom. Never place running water in the bedroom—too much chi energy disturbs the sleep. This includes heavy turbulent water pictures as well.

Also, place items in this sector that symbolize fun and happiness, such as pictures of family outings, hobbies, or recreation. To bring in good health in abundance, place bowls of fruit or pictures of objects that depict a healthy lifestyle.

Place travel brochures in this area if you wish to travel and do so in abundance. Use your imagination. Expand your horizons and fly in this sector. This sector is not just about money. Use metal sparingly in this direction.

Use items in this gua that make you feel abundant. Use expensive furniture or new towels and sheets, or expensive perfume and lotions. Use expensive candles made with soy and natural scents. Splurge on new clothes, especially underwear, because it is closest to the body. Start acting as though you are abundant.

Always enhance the energy of the space with mirrors and crystals to double abundance and disperse it out into other areas of your life.

If this area is a storage place, make sure it is clear and free of clutter. Maybe put an Intention Box or collage of those things you wish to manifest in this area.

Do not place garbage cans, cat boxes, clutter, or cremation ashes in this sector.

External Recognition (Fame)—South/Li

After we accumulate riches in our life, next comes our external recognitions or fame sector of the south. External recognition or fame is ruled by fire and is located in the south and associated with the number 9 of expansion in the Lo-Shu square. The south home is a Li facing/Kan sitting home. The south sector is associated with and fortunate for the middle daughter. The middle daughter or middle-aged woman will find power in this sector and may wish to locate her office or bedroom here when the annual flying star is auspicious.

This space represents our reputation, integrity, and notability. This is where we become recognized for our accomplishments, whether we are a mother or the president of the United States—after all, even he or she had a mother.

This is the area in our home in which we can accomplish our goals and dreams. It is the sector of fame, good fortune, and goal setting. Get your head in the right place. All is possible. Thoughts spring forth into action. You are the force and mind behind all recognition.

Display items that will aspire, inspire, and energize you. People who live in south-facing houses tend to be higher profile people or people in higher-profile jobs. Hang certificates or recognition in this space with a light above them. Use jewel-tone colors in this space, especially red and purple.

Since the horse rules the south, you may wish to place horses running in from the south direction. Always place the horse energy running into the home toward the center of the home. Do not point out a window or door.

Display mementos from those expressing admiration, gratitude, or love—such as children's drawings, thank-you notes, or invitations—in this sector.

Fire energy includes warmth, lighting, candles, incense, pointed objects, or other fire symbols. Chinese red lanterns or firecrackers especially enhance this area. Incorporate triangles, geometric designs, or pyramid shapes.

Use metal sparingly in this direction and avoid metal wind chimes. Bamboo wind chimes may be used in the place of metal chimes.

Intimate Relations—Southwest/Kun

The cycle of life continues forward from the external recognition to the intimacy sector. Here is housed the desire to connect to the Earth and those around us. This sector also represents self-trust, self-love, and self-esteem. It houses your relationship to anything you manifest on an intimate level, whether it be a spouse, your children, a job, or even an idea. It is a commitment to this specific person, place, or idea.

The intimacy area is usually indicative of a couple's reality; it is devoted to love and support between two people. The intimacy sector is a place where you can develop emotionally, sexually, and spiritually as a couple. However, this space can be used to develop intimacy with those around us, such as parents and children.

Use this space to learn to trust yourself. This space can be used to develop intimacy with the spiritual realm. Use the spiritual guidance of this space to understand better those with whom you are close, whether spouse, family, or friend. Lack of understanding comes from lack of communication with the source of the problem.

The intimacy sector is ruled by small/feminine earth and is represented in the Lo-Shu square by the number 2 of relationships. The southwest home is called Kun facing/Ken sitting. This sector is strong for mother or woman. When the annual flying star is auspicious, the mother or woman may wish to locate her office or bedroom in this area.

Arrange items of romance or love in this area. Place rose quartz, Mandarin ducks, flowers, pink or red crystals, groupings of two to symbolize couples, and pink peonies in the southwest.

However, if your southwest area is the kitchen or middle of the home, be creative with these ideas. These adjustments can also apply to the bedroom area, no matter in which direction it may be located. It is important to pay attention to self.

You can also use art, photographs, or anything that symbolizes romance or intimacy to you. In your bedroom, hang pictures of lovers or images that depict two people. Avoid solitary beings unless you are healing from a previous relationship. If healing from a relationship, place pictures of single people in this area until the time comes to find another relationship. This will help you find comfort in solitude.

Do not use images that appear lonely or depressing. Always ask yourself, "What does this picture symbolize to me?" Group objects in pairs if you are looking for romance. Do not hang pictures of children or parents in the bedroom because, subconsciously, you may feel they are watching and know what you are doing.

If you are seeking intimacy with a spouse, buy new underwear and lingerie to make yourself feel sexier. It is hard to feel sexy in flannel or cotton granny underwear. Wear silk or try new thong underwear. Be daring when it comes to undergarments. Remember, they are really more for you than they are for your spouse. Go through your closet and get rid of all that does not represent who you want to be. Be adventurous. Dare to be naughty.

Always sleep on cotton sheets and in natural sleepwear. Synthetic fabrics do not resonate as well with your body energies. Sleeping in the nude is ideal because it allows the body to breathe. The body is free and released to rejuvenate and energize.

Use this area to engage your root chakra. A happy root chakra is necessary for grounding the whole body (refer to section on root chakra). Dance, play, and have sex in this sector. Get reacquainted with your body and your spouse's body.

If there is no one special in your life but you wish there to be, hang a pink crystal here to attract that special someone. Activate the area as if two people already live there. Place pictures of couples here. Do not place pictures of solitary individuals if you are looking for a spouse. It sends the message to the subconscious mind that you wish to remain solo.

Children's bedrooms should be separate from a parent's space. A parent's bedroom should be off limits to children, unless permission is provided. Do not allow toys, cribs, or laundry here. Boundaries should be set to keep the intimacy area sacred only to the couple. Bonding with a child is fine; however, parents and children need their own space to recognize independence.

Place no treadmills, computers, or work-related items in this area. This area is for relaxation and rejuvenation.

Avoid large, intrusive objects in this sector. Keep the décor softer with soft, flowing furnishings and lots of pillows to promote relaxation. Use luxurious items. This area needs to feel special.

Make use of pastel or warm colors. Pink or silver is good in this space. Purple is a harmonizing color, but avoid peach. Peach is a color of change and can cause emotions to waver. Stay away from it in the intimacy area.

In this space, feature reminders of things you have experienced together as a couple, such as photographs from a favorite performance, dinner, or a vacation. However, never put items from an outing taken with others here. This initiates development of intimacy with people other than your spouse. (Unless that is what you wish to do.)

Creativity (Offspring, Children, Ideas)—West/Tui

Our journey begins at birth. We have to learn about life and find our family roots and belief systems. From those beliefs, we develop wealth, reputation, and commitment. This commitment's time has come in the west in the form of children, ideas, or the creative arts, such as music, drama, and fine arts.

The west is represented by Joyous Lake and the metal lake. It is represented by the number 7 in the original Lo-Shu square. The west home is called Tui facing/Chen sitting.

The west sector is associated with and fortunate for the youngest daughter. The youngest daughter or young woman will find power in this sector and may wish to locate her office or bedroom here when the annual flying star is auspicious.

This sector represents creativity, children, ideas, and happiness. This also represents the playground of childhood. Use this area to dance, laugh, play, have sex, and really explore what you want to be when you grow up. It is a place to explore, play, create, let the imagination run wild, pursue creative interests, or initiate your child's creativity.

Realize that your goals may change several times in your lifetime. This is the place to develop goals and dreams. Use this space to create, recreate yourself, and generally space out in. This may be the area of the home to consider and evaluate if you wish to conceive a child. Meditate in this area to enhance your dreams into reality. Children and adults need a space like this just to have fun. Paint, spill, laugh, and jump. Keep this area playful, light, and fun. This is a great place to display whimsical décor, such as fairies, unicorns, wizards, etc.

The west represents "of the mind"—creating, inventing, and researching. This area is associated with the psyche, or mental well-being. Fun and games represent happiness. All work and no play represent low feelings. If the psyche is low, creativity is low. Use rainbow colors to raise the creativity energy. Use gemstones or semiprecious stones to symbolize the rainbow colors. Use metallic colors such as those found in Mardi Gras beads. Use mirrors or still water in this area.

Be careful, though, of an imbalance of metal in this area. It can become rigid and cold feeling. Control the sharp energy of metal with a little bit of blue, AB crystals, or clear or small blue crystals. Use leaded crystals or mobiles to bring rainbow light into the room.

The west is a great place to locate a child's playroom. Display children's photographs or artwork in this area. Round objects symbolize metal. Use a piggy bank full of coins to inspire and motivate. Children love money and what it can get them.

Incorporate objects or symbols representing your gifts to the world or what you would like your gifts to the world to be. Remember—if you can dream it, you can be it.

Benefactors/Travel/Spiritual—Northwest/Chien

The eighth and final sector of the ba gua is known as the benefactors sector. This area is associated with the northwest and is symbolic of heaven, father, and the mind. It can also be associated with mentors, travel, community, and religious or spiritual beliefs. The northwest is ruled by metal and is associated with the number 6 of the original Lo-Shu square. The northwest home is Chien facing/Sun sitting. The patriarchal male may wish to locate his office or bedroom in this sector when the annual flying star is auspicious.

Your journey or purpose within your home ends in void of the northwest, which lies between the west of endings and the north of beginnings. This sector symbolizes the completeness of the journey of a particular situation in a home. A home may hold the energy for the lessons of health challenges, career or money successes or failures, relationship failure or successes, or family successes and failures. No matter what the lesson, you are in a specific home for a specific reason, and that lesson will be completed in that residence.

Once the lessons are learned in a specific area of your life, you will feel the need to move on and away from the energy that held it in place. You become antsy. After a certain lesson in a home is complete, people have been known to leave careers, relationships, and sometimes even marriages behind.

A style of home tells the story of the purpose of the house and why its occupants may be drawn to it. The main floor represents the now, the second floor represents the future, and the basement of the home represents the past. Unfortunately, the basement types may have trouble letting go of the past. These individuals need to be especially diligent in keeping the basement clean and free of excess clutter to keep moving forward in their lives.

For instance, a young couple may be attracted to a two story-home to accommodate their future children and an active social life. This home serves, through the years, as a base for the children to grow. The basement may also have become a gathering place for the lifetime of memories for the couple and their children. As the children grow and leave home and the couple becomes less active and more inclined to prefer quiet, the large home has reached the pinnacle of its usefulness.

The house may begin to become a burden with the memories and patterns from the past, the energy of the now, and the changes needed for the future. Some may choose to hold on tightly to the past and the memories, while others may find they wish to sell or remodel their homes to remodel themselves.

You may live several journeys within the same home. When the old purpose is complete and your new journey is ready to begin, it is important to redirect and recreate the home to fit each new purpose. You cannot continue to do the same thing over and over and expect different results. Following the old patterns of behavior when the new ones are trying to emerge is futile and exhausting. Teachers will always appear to take you to the next level when you are ready, and with each journey, you will see through different eyes. This completion is called the journey of the ba gua.

This area also represents the ability to interact with others. It is our ability to give and receive aid when it is needed along life's path. It represents the people who help us in life and those we have helped or will help. It represents our connection to a universal life force, something outside of ourselves that provides a positive, helpful influence. It is all our visible and invisible means of support, whether it be Jesus, God, Buddha, a spirit guide, a relative who has gone before us, or a living person. This sector corresponds to our sense of community and how we fit into its structure. It is also strongly connected to travel.

As a learning tool, this sector can be used to increase spiritual connection, develop psychic energy, find teachers or mentors, connect to your higher God, and engage in physical or astral travel.

Place spiritual items in this gua to represent your connection to another plane, according to your belief. Consider placing pictures of Jesus, Buddha, Mother Mary, White Tara, and/or Kwan Yin, statues of angels, spirit guides, or deceased relatives who supported you in life in this area to enhance feelings of enlightenment. Display pictures, books, or mementos of mentors and teachers who have influenced you.

For business, the northwest symbolizes clients coming to you. Put objects in this space that represent your clients or potential clients. You may wish to place your address book, laptop, or a telephone in the northwest of an office or home.

Group items in threes or more to represent community—stay away from solitary items or pairs. Also, add items symbolic of events in which you participate or want to participate. Hang mirrors to encourage communication on a physical and spiritual level. Place yellow, purple, or clear crystals in this area to enhance its energy.

If you wish to travel, display items of your travels or travel brochures of places you wish to visit. Place your luggage in this area.

Use grays, silver, and gold in this area, as well as anything metal.

Center (Health and Good Luck)

The health center is the center of the home. Keep this sector as clear of clutter as possible. The health center should have no bathrooms, stairs, or closets. If there are bathrooms, hang a crystal in the bathroom to raise chi. If there is a staircase in the middle of the home, hang a crystal at the top of the stairs to stabilize chi. If there are closets in the center of the home, make certain the closets are organized and clear of clutter to ensure the chi can flow in and out.

To enhance chi in the center of the home, hang an attractive light fixture with crystals in this area. A ceiling fan will help to circulate chi throughout the home. Place the setting on low at all times. Be sure no furniture is located directly under the fan. A fan's current disturbs the chi of the body and can cause short-term weakness and fatigue. If you must use furniture in this space, make sure it allows the chi to flow around it or through it. Stickley style or wicker furniture is the best to use.

To make accurate corrections to the home, use the yearly annual star adjustments associated with the number in the center.

Additional Feng Shui Tips

To prevent backstabbing and gossip, place a rooster at your front door or near your desk.

For protection from robbery or negative energy, place three ki luns, two fu dogs, or a compass or a line of salt at your front door or in the directions of the negative annual flying stars.

For career success, display the golden monkey on a horse in your favorable career direction or the north of the home.

Everyone should always display his or her personal Chinese animal—based upon the year he or she was born—in the direction of its power.

Peach Blossom Secret for Love

The term peach blossom is be used to enhance love activity. Too much peach blossom can result in sex or extramarital affairs, so one needs to be careful how it is applied.

If your year animal is a rat, dragon, or monkey, place a golden rooster in the west. If you are a tiger, horse, or dog, place a green rabbit in the east. If you are a snake, ox, or rooster, place a red horse in the south. If you are a rabbit, sheep, or pig, place a blue rat in the north.

You may also activate the peach blossom by placing rose quartz, a pink rotating crystal, pink lotus, pairs of birds such as ducks or lovebirds, and pink peony flowers in your bedroom or peach blossom direction.

Leaded Feng Shui Crystals

For stale energy use, crystals should be hung from the ceiling to ensure upward energy movement. Each crystal holds a different property of energy, as follows:

Pink—Love

Purple—Spirituality/Mystical/Intuition

Red—Fire/Energy/Sex

Peach—Romance/Beauty

Clear/White—Clarity/Insight

Blue—Water/Calming/Clearing

Green—Wood/Healing/Growth

Yellow—Money/Grounding

Feng Shui Rule

Always balance all five elements within the home. Make certain there is a balance of the water, wood, fire, earth, and metal elements. Balance the yin and yang elements of the home. This promotes harmony and balance, similar to that found in nature.

The condition of our home has a direct effect on the health of our mind, body, and spirit. You are your home, and your home is a reflection of you. What do you want that reflection to be?

Space Clearing

Space clearing is needed to eliminate or resonate energetic life forms that become attached to the energy fields of people, animals, land, and buildings. Sometimes, whole neighborhoods, villages, or countries can be affected by the invasion of this energy.

Some entities may be spirits or ghosts of those who have died but have failed to pass over because of trauma or strife. Some are frightened, others may be angry, and some are just lost or confused.

Space clearing can also be used to shift energy created by our behavior and decisions made in this life or from a past life. Negative past experiences affect our beliefs and decisions, thus attracting more of these experiences to us like a magnet. Patterns, once created and accepted by the body, take on a life of their own. When we try to change these behaviors, this energy may become uncomfortable with the new energetic behavior pattern we are trying to create. This old energy begins to feel like a ghost of our past—haunting us, trying to pull us back into the old patterns. This stagnant lingering energy can affect our ability to move forward as quickly as we would like with a clear vision of the future. When this confusion occurs, the need for space clearing or ghost busting of the physical body and environment begins.

Throughout the ages, the power of rituals has been a part of traditional Chinese feng shui, as well as of other cultures. Native Americans, Egyptians, Greeks, Chinese, Mayans, and many others have used the power of the clearing and cleansing rituals to get rid of evil spirits or perceived evil spirits and to balance the person or space with a renewal of energies.

There are several methods of space clearing that are quite effective. I will offer a few of my favorites. However, this is not an accurate science. Each individual has the inherent power to develop effective space clearing techniques for himself or herself. The following is just a guideline.

Clearing should be done in the yin of the afternoon or p.m. hours. The best time for the yin hour is from 9:00 p.m. to 1:00 a.m. Magic keepers of old did these rituals between 11:30 p.m. and 12:30 a.m. The midnight hour is the "Garden of Good and Evil."

The bag of tools you will need includes the following:

- A toning instrument, a drum, a hand chime, or a toning bowl
- Anointing oil or a blend of orange and frankincense oils mixed with bottled water in a spray bottle*
- Incense—either sage, lemongrass, sweet grass, frankincense, or another scent that is acceptable for clearing and refreshing the air*
- Candles—one white and one black; small votive or mini candle

**You may use either the oil or incense. Both are acceptable.*

To prepare for a space clearing or ghost-busting experience, shower before beginning the space-clearing work to remove all energy of your day and to renew and cleanse the body. Wear washable, 100 percent natural fabrics.

Clear your energy field of all debris, negativity, and stress. Never space clear when you are ill or feeling tired. This will only serve to make you more fatigued. In old cultures, women never performed this ritual if they were menstruating. The blood is considered unclean because it is being cast from the body. Menstruation was believed to put women in a weakened physical state.

Dress in something comfortable, loose fitting, and made of 100 percent natural fabrics that allow your body to breathe and work more intuitively and without restriction. At the end of the clearing, it is important to wash your clothing and shower off immediately.

Meditate:

Before placing yourself within the energy of the person or space, meditate for at least fifteen minutes. Clear your mind, body, and spirit through breathing techniques. Ask your angels, protectors, teachers, and guardians to come with you to help in your work. You may ask for the Archangel Michael to protect and assist you. Ask for the proper intuition level to assist you in your task of clearing in accordance with the divine plan. Anoint yourself with frankincense oil or smudge yourself with sage to protect you from any unwanted energy or attachment. Repeat a prayer of your choice nine times. Or you may wish to repeat the traditional feng shui prayer—Ohm Ma Ne Pad Me Hum (nine times).

As you begin, light the black candle to dissolve all negativity and darkness within the home. Light the white candle so the spirits can find their way to the light. Light the incense, as the smoke is the direction to the heavens so the spirits can find their way.

Begin at the front door—open the door. Open all curtains or blinds so the sunlight or moonlight can enter. Open the windows, especially if the home smells musty. Yin spirits of the darkness like dark and musty areas. Do this in each room if necessary.

Yin spirits tend to hide in the southwest and northeast of the home because of the heavy earth energy. Make sure these areas of the home are well lighted and airy. There should be no wind chimes in these directions because chimes may stir up yin energies.

As you begin your journey through the home, spray or smudge the front door. If you anoint it with oil, spray all corners of the front door. If you feel so compelled, take droplets of oil and place them on all corners of the front door, inside and out. If you are using sage or incense, make sure the smoke lingers at the door, first on the outside and then on the inside. Next, ring a chime or tone of some kind at the front door, inside and out. Make sure this area is clear because the front door is the mouth of chi or the energy coming in the door.

Continue through the home in a clockwise direction. Spray, smudge, or anoint all windows as you go. Again, if the room seems stuffy, open the windows. This allows fresh air in and negative energy to exit. Leave them open as you circulate through the home. Ring the chime in each room and in the corners of neglect. Cobwebs are indicative of stale energy. After you have worked the room, stand at its center and make a figure eight infinity symbol to indicate the completeness of being in accordance with the divine purpose.

After you have gone through the home, including the basement, go back and close the windows. Now you are going to stabilize the energy with a positive force. Spray the frankincense/orange oils again throughout the home, or burn an incense of orange, lemongrass, or saffron. You want to replace the smell of the home with something indicative of pleasure and happiness . . . something euphoric.

As you finish clearing the home, be sure to clear yourself and the home's occupants with the frankincense spray or smudge.

Go back to the altar, and see if the candles have burned down. You may notice that the black candle burned quickly, while the white candle is lingering in essence. Say your prayer of thanks and your chant of Ohm Ma Ne Pad Me Hum—nine times. Take a deep breath, clear your mind, and then excuse yourself from the home.

Upon returning home, take another shower or bath, cleaning and clearing all entity residue off you. Wash all clothes.

Meditate again, thanking the heavens for your wonderful life and profession.

Ohm, Ma, Ne, Pad, Me, Hum—May peace be with you.

Part

FOUR

Chakras and How They Relate to the Body, Home, and Health

To begin your path to understanding the deeper meaning of developing your quantum mind ability, you must first familiarize yourself with how your mind, body, spirit, past programming, and environment relate to each other. The body must be at optimum energy with your mind alert and your environment stable.

The belief in a higher power that works with you to guide your destiny is important to the success of manifesting your desires. Get connected to your spiritual beliefs, whether you call it God, Buddha, nature, or Yoda from *Star Wars*. It doesn't matter what you call it; what does matter is that you believe there is a higher place from which you receive innate information on a moment-to-moment basis.

Peace and harmony within your life begin with your body. As you begin your journey into the feng shui of your life, your body is the first place to start. You have been told since childhood to eat right, exercise, and get adequate rest. These really are the keys to good mental and physical health. Although we have heard these often, we do not always understand the true significance or depth of their importance. As life becomes increasingly busy, stressed, and cluttered, we search for ways to ease the discomfort. Instead of exercising and resting properly, some may overeat or use alcohol or prescription drugs while others may smoke cigarettes or pot in an attempt to help cope with hectic schedules or cluttered lifestyles. Some may indulge in addictions to gambling, sex, shopping, etc.

Unfortunately, these coping methods have the opposite effect, causing the energy system to malfunction. The system may become sluggish or lethargic, often losing touch with happiness, passion for life, health, productivity, creativity, and true sexual desire. The outlook on life becomes labored, and life becomes a struggle instead of a pleasure. When the guiding faith in a higher power becomes cloudy and the messages from our spirit become muted or confusing, a lack of faith sets in, and hopelessness is the outcome. Because of this stress, goals and dreams take a backseat to basic survival.

When this happens, the mind becomes confused, and sufferers will often allow other people to make decisions for them because they don't have the spiritual will or trust to make the decisions for themselves. They often settle for less—doing only what they think they are supposed to do. Some may stay in a job they don't like because it is too scary to find another, while others may stay in a bad relationship because it is familiar and breaking up is too hard. When unhappy conditions persists over a period of time, breakdown within a chakra area can occur, and physical illness results.

The body knows when it is out of balance and harmony with our higher goals, and our bodies will become sick or sad to get our attention. When disease affects the body, it is a message to pay attention to emotional or spiritual desires. For these reasons, it is so important to eat right with proper nutrition, get rest and exercise, and keep our spiritual convictions intact.

God meant for all of us—not just a chosen few—to be successful, beautiful, healthy, and happy. Get clear on your soul's purpose or life's path. Begin your journey right now. Begin aligning your chakras through exercise; access God, your guides, and your inner voice through meditation; and remember to keep a journal of all experiences that are representations or manifestations that you are on the right path.

Exercise helps move energy throughout the body. The body must be supplied with fresh air and nutrition. Exercise increases oxygen and circulation to the muscles, blood, nerves, tissues, and fibers of the body. Only with exercise is the body truly awakened to do its job efficiently. Toxins are eliminated, and the body is allowed to function properly. When the body feels healthy and happy, thinking becomes clearer, and goals and life purpose become apparent. Spiritually, we feel complete.

We all may find completeness several times within our lifetime. Once a goal is met, a new one will be established. The body is a survivor. It will continue seeking things to make it feel better and find balance again. This is why people sometimes ask, "Aren't you ever satisfied?" The proper response is, "No, because I am alive and always seeking." As we grow and change, passions change. That is the tai chi of life—growth and change. Embrace it.

As passions change, so must your physical environment. If the mind and body change but the physical environment remains the same, change will not occur as quickly. This stuck, stagnant energy of the environment will cause a cycle of frustration and the body will become out of sync with the mind.

The mind, body, and home must reflect who we are and portray the message we are sending the world as the reflection of our being. The home can help to make the body and mind stronger by supporting the energy centers or chakras of the body.

The word *chakra* is Sanskrit for "energy center." The chakras regulate the chi flow or energy that moves in and out of our bodies and coincides with our endocrine system. The chakras are directly related to the five elements of earth, water, wood (air), fire, and metal (ether).

Each chakra, although ruled by a major element, must have the other elements in balance for creation (water), action (wood), passion (fire), order (metal), and support (earth). As we learn to keep the elements balanced in the chakras of our body, we must also balance the elements within our home. We can truly change our existence as the body balance and the home balance maintain equilibrium. It is especially important to understand the grounding of the root chakra and the vast effect it has upon our being.

The body has seven major chakras and twenty-one minor chakras. In Chinese medicine, these are called meridian points. The points of the major chakras are the same as the conception vessel and the governing vessels in Chinese medicine.

The major chakras are located at the pubic bone (root), a couple of inches below the navel (spleen), a couple of inches above the navel (solar plexus), the heart, the throat, the middle of the forehead (third eye), and the top of the head (crown).

The minor chakras are the energy meridian points along the body. These points are important to know because each conveys a daily message from our physical body to our mind. One is located in front of each ear, one above each breast, one where the clavicles meet, one in each palm of the hand, one on the sole of each foot, one just behind each eye, one related to each gonad, one near the liver, one connected with the stomach, two connected with the spleen, one behind each knee, and one near the solar plexus.

Seven Major Chakras

First Chakra—Root Chakra

Kundalini Fire Energy

Throughout ancient times, the root chakra has been associated with the dragon and the snake energy. The kundalini energy literally means "coiled" and is envisioned as a sleeping serpent at the base of the spine. When awakened through exercise or meditation, the kundalini energy snakes throughout our entire being, bringing forth a heightened state of awareness and bliss. As the root chakra awakens and new neuro-path ways open, one may experience new and different body sensations such as vision changes with bright lights and floaters, enhanced hearing, psychic enhancement, and transcendental experiences.

The root chakra is located on the pubic bone in the front of the body and extends internally through the body to the base of the spine on the back of the body. The root chakra is associated with the base of the spine, genitals, large intestines, legs, feet, bones, and teeth. Health issues associated with the root chakra are spine problems (support), arthritis, sciatica, knee problems, foot problems, hemorrhoids, and constipation.

This chakra is your foundation, your support system, and your main energy center in life. It relates to survival and houses the fight or flight response. The root chakra is responsible for your sense of grounding to the earth in the physical plane. Passion, sexuality, sensuality, security, physical energy, health, vitality, and anything that is connected to the physical world—the items you can touch—are housed in root chakra energy. The root chakra is the center of manifestation. Your root chakra, when strong and stable, brings to you an abundance of the wealth, health, and happiness that you strive to find in your life.

The root chakra must first be stabilized before the other chakras can follow. Think of it in pictures. If you have a building with six floors constructed on a strong foundation, what happens to the stability of the upper floors? They stay strong. However, if the top six floors are built upon a weak foundation, the building will sway and become more unstable with each moving or upheaval energy of the Earth.

The body operates in the exact same way. When the root chakra is strong, so are the other six chakras. The energy moving into them is solid. This energy, strong or weak, will affect every aspect of the organs and their function, quality of thinking and security, health, physical strength, psychic intuitions, memory, communication, and much more.

To stabilize and strengthen the root chakra, you must engage in physical activities. As the physical strength becomes stronger, the chakra moves more easily, and other areas of the body begin responding. Simple exercise is all that is needed to activate and charge the root chakra. This should come as no surprise because for years doctors have told us of the benefits of exercise. Now is the time to take heed and do it.

The root chakra is ruled by fire energy that stirs your desires. The fire energy blends into earth energy, grounding your passions. The earth energy is similar to gravity, the stability and foundation that holds you in place. However, it is always important to understand what ideas or desires you are grounding. Make sure they are the ones you desire. Always focus on the positive of the situation.

The root chakra is associated with the northeast or the self-knowledge sector of the ba gua. Self-knowledge is the discovery of who and what you and your belief system truly are. It is your foundation of confidence, past experiences, and influences. The root chakra holds your ability to manifest and gather those physical things in life you need.

Use tones of browns or yellows to ground the root chakra. Use red to uplift and activate the root chakra. Because the earth element controls water, the kidneys and bladder may become involved. Use blue, black, or water elements to help bring balance to the root chakra. This chakra of the northeast of self-knowledge then blends into the family sector associated with wood, which in turn is associated with the east sector of the home in the ba gua. As we are born into a family, that family takes care of us and imprints us with their beliefs, relationships, social status, and journey or career from their frame of reference. Through this growth, we develop trust, love, and confidence from their perspective. We then leave our tribe to develop and ground our own being, our own self-love, self-trust, and self-confidence. The problem is whether your desires match those of your imprinting. If not, conflict of self ensues.

When the root chakra is balanced, we possess a centered, grounded feeling. We know what is right for us and are able to express it clearly. We feel healthy and have an abundance of physical and sexual energy. We experience an increased sensation of touch, movement, and kinesthetic presence. Kinesthetic feelings in the body are feelings of balance, shivers, hair standing on end, energy running through the body, and physical pleasure or pain.

When there is uncertainty in the root chakra, energy may be weak and a tendency toward becoming ill easily exists. When one feels insecure in his or her familial learning foundation, he or she may have a strong desire to search for answers outside the safety zone. However, there may be an innate fear of leaving the familiar for the unknown, which may incapacitate you. Questions of doubt, trust, and capabilities may arise. Quality of character surfaces, and conflicts between what you know and what you would like for yourself come up. This fear may breed selfishness, jealousy, and greediness. Earth's output energy of metal is needed to bring order to the chaos. Wear metal jewelry and take vitamin supplements if needed.

If your moods are severely out of balance, get your adrenal glands and hormones tested. Get blood and saliva tests done to have the information you need to chemically come back into alignment. They are good hormone-balancing and replacement therapies available.

Overactivity in the root chakra may also cause increased sexual energy without emotional attachment. A tendency toward promiscuous sex, illicit sex, or pornography may surface. Suicidal tendencies may also become known. Apply water to balance the root chakra's frustrated energy. Water is associated with calm, restoration, and sexual organs. Water is the wealth of the earth element, and it softens energy from the earth element, causing the earth to move and regenerate. Metal is the output of the earth element, and it is needed to recognize and relieve the stored sexual energy. Metal is also associated with sexual desire. In essence, water and metal are needed energetically to balance the cycle of the loving emotions and sexual desire.

When ungrounded or confused about your life's journey, use the northeast sector of the ba gua in combination with the chakra-balancing meditations to help get the answers for which you are searching. Remember, the answers come one step at a time and in the time frame you are able to understand and process them. Everything happens for a reason. There are no coincidences. Don't force destiny; let it unfold for you.

When in a state of instability or confusion, pay attention to the condition of the northeast sector/self-knowledge sector of the ba gua. Make sure this area is clear of all clutter, has open spaces, and is light and airy.

Ask yourself, "What are my goals? What do I need to be happy and successful?" The northeast or self-discovery sector will help you discover the life choices available to you. Closely examine your current life choices and determine whether they fit your desires and dreams. If they do not, start activating the northeast sector of your home with the intentions you wish to manifest, and use design items to anchor those manifestations. Get that root chakra into balance through meditation, so the mind and physical body can begin working together in perfect harmony.

Some meditation practices to strengthen the root chakra may include walking meditations or surrendering yourself to a relaxing massage.

Address your issues, if any, of degradation and shame of self—sexually. Get to know your body better than anyone else does. Make peace with yourself and those around you. Make love to your partner to relieve stresses and tension and to open the root chakra to enjoy life to its fullest. Teach your mate what you desire sexually. Find a balance for your partner and yourself.

Dancing, playing, physical exercise, making love, going barefoot, gardening, and cooking are all great grounding exercises. Be still afterwards and pay attention to what messages or epiphanies come during the relaxation process. It may surprise you what you have been trying so hard to control. Ask for what you want. You deserve a happy life. Once your root chakra is functioning at optimum level, so will the rest of your life. It will happen when you are not looking.

To begin chakra work, sit down in the northeast of your home. Use this area to face and release your fears and ground your being. Get clear on what you need to do to feel secure in your life and to achieve your goals. Learn independence in this area.

Prepare yourself with the mudra. Recite the sound associated with the root chakra, and then recite the affirmation. You may use the stones or oils also associated with the chakra to enhance energy. Focus all your attention upon grounding your energy and any other questions that may come up for you. When you are finished, be sure to journal and log your progress. If you do not, you will forget the messages that were given to you.

Mudra for the root chakra for universal energy and eternity

Sit with a straight spine with your legs crossed in front of you. Bend your elbows and open your arms out to the side at heart level. Keep palms facing up to the heavens with the fingers close together. Concentrate on the root chakra and feel a silver light energy coming from the earth through the root chakra, up the spine of the body, and into the heart chakra. At the same time, feel a gold light energy from the heavens coming into the crown chakra on the top of the head and moving down the body into the heart chakra. As the two meet at the heart chakra, relax and feel a sense of peace from Mother Earth and Father Sky. Breathe long deep breaths in the nose and out the mouth while reciting the sound associated with the root chakra. The sound associated with the root chakra is "OH."

(See photo of mudra on page 138.)

Mudra for root, spleen, or solar plexus chakra to conquer fear, abuse, and trauma

Bend your elbow and place your left hand, facing upward, halfway between the root chakra and the solar plexus chakra. The left hand symbolizes receiving courage and strength. Place your right hand, with palm turned outward, out to the side of your body, bent in toward the shoulder. The right hand symbolizes divine protection. This mudra will help diminish fear. Breathe in your nose and out your mouth, long deep breaths, while reciting the root mantra—"OH."

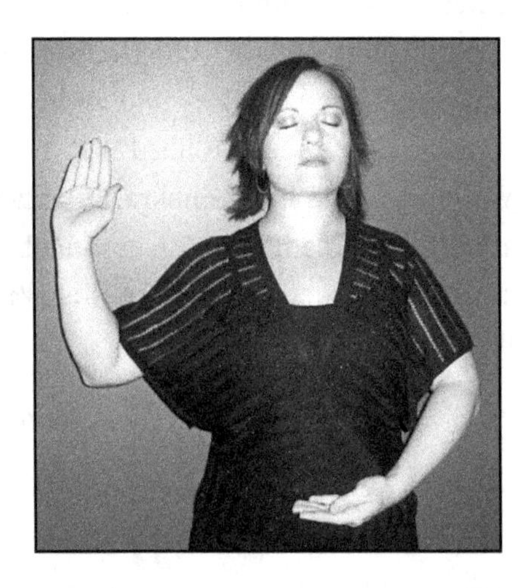

Affirmation for the root chakra

"I am grounded, secure, and able to make my own choices. I am brave."

Essential oils for the root chakra

Cinnamon: Stimulates sex organs and potency

Ginger: Endows physical energy

Geranium: Used for clearing stress

Basil: Clears the head and relieves mental fatigue

Pepper: Helps maintain stamina and energy; supports the intestinal tract

Patchouli: Tonic and stimulant

Vetiver: Grounds and calms the body

Note: If you are pregnant or nursing, taking medication, or under a doctor's care, be sure to discuss the oils' interactions with the doctor.

Stones that support the root chakra

Agates: Offers strength, protection, and support

Ruby: Increases stability in economic status; worn to enhance physical beauty and endurance

Garnet: Encourages success in business

Bloodstone: Provides strength and courage

Black Tourmaline: Stimulates direction, achievement, and positive actions

Smoky Quartz: Generates energy for added boost

Coral: Encourages physical stamina

Hematite: Gives protection from negative influences

Kyanite: Repels negativity

Labradorite: Grounds; helps to line up chakras; relieves shaking or nervous conditions

Root chakra strengthening exercise

The purpose of this exercise is to open up the kundalini energy and allow energy to flow through the root chakra area to increase that passion, playfulness, and sensuality. When our security, lifestyle, or belief system has been threatened, the root chakra will overtax and decline trying to protect and defend our being. Because of this factor, over time, many women and men will develop a weakened root chakra. Get your adrenals and hormones checked if you find you are fatigued with sleeping interruptions.

Woman are especially prone to this aspect. When a woman becomes a wife or mother, often the definition of how she views herself changes dramatically. She may change from being carefree and self-centered to becoming a spouse. As a wife, she may feel she is now expected to take care of her husband and his needs and demands, often at the expense of her own. This leaves little or no time for self-inquiry or reflection.

The woman, of course, may resent this, but in part she is responsible for it. It is the role she has accepted and is the message she is sending back to others in a physical form. If this should occur, she needs to find a balance between self, husband, family, and career.

When women become mothers, the feeling of sensuality and sexuality may begin to wane, and personal passions take a back seat to the more day-to-day household duties. On top of that, many are working a forty-hour-a-week job as well. Laughter, sexual pleasure, dancing, and looking and feeling good seem to fade and become distant memories as the tired woman may become more matronly, taking care of the required daily tasks of work and home. She may tend to gain weight because of the added burden and a lack of attention and comfort given to herself. To offset this tendency, she could perhaps allow her family some independence in their ability to care for some of the household responsibilities.

The root chakra, as well as the spleen chakra, becomes a place of pain many times during a woman's lifetime. It begins with menstruation, accommodates pregnancy and childbirth, and ends with menopause.

Postpartum depression is a classic example of root chakra breakdown because of the trauma of childbirth affecting the hormones of the other chakras. A great number of women through their lifetimes will disconnect from this area, which in turn disconnects from the pleasure and the passion of the root chakra and the ability to bond with others. Sex may no longer be a pleasure but a burden. Time and energy for sex becomes a job, much like the laundry, cooking, and cleaning. Sensuality and looking good are no longer a priority. These aspects may equally apply when disappointments in relationships hurt the self-esteem.

In addition, the media constantly sends the message that once a female becomes a wife or a mother or reaches a certain age, she is no longer attractive and should put aside the desire and passions of the younger or single women. I was once told, "Women over fifty are invisible." I was shocked, and I declared to myself, "I will never become invisible!"

Both women and men can become victims of society or advertising, but only if we allow these exterior forces to hypnotize or have power over us. Although primarily for women, an excellent book on the subject is *Deadly Persuasion: Why Women and Girls Must Fight the Addictive Power of Advertising*, by Jean Kilbourne and Mary Pipher. If you feel you are being overly influenced by advertising and media, this book helps identify powerful addictive messages and the subliminal techniques employed to send them.

Media advertising preys on all of us, especially women and girls, sending the message that they must be dangerously thin, smoke, drink, or party to be attractive. The typical woman of average weight and size begins to question her ability to be attractive, sexy, or desirable when she has to compete with what the media portrays as the "perfect woman."

Advertising insinuates that the average woman is a size 0. I once owned a dress store, and found the average teenage girl was a size 12 to 14, and the average shoe size was an 8. Unfortunately, these beautiful girls felt inferior to their size 0 counterparts. The result is that women will often shut down when criticized and give up on themselves and their romance, passion, and sexuality. They begin to feel "less than."

As a hypnotherapist, I often work with clients on self-esteem issues. In my opinion, this type of "to be perfect" media pressure may be consciously or subconsciously the cause of the increased use of legal and illegal drugs and alcohol among women. It may also explain the increase in cases of anorexia and bulimia in both women and men and might be responsible for some of the deaths caused by diet pills and surgeries to aid in weight loss. These problems need to be viewed as a real epidemic in the United States, especially when the problems surface among the youngest and most vulnerable. I have seen it affect girls as young as nine. Sadly, society accepts it as so. It truly is time to speak up and protect these children and women from society's pressure.

We must all take responsibility for our decisions. We need to be aware of the outside influences such as advertising that take away our sense of who we are and what is right and normal for us. We need to reground ourselves often by finding what is right for us and then taking part in those activities. Be proud of who you are and what you do. If you are not, simply readjust what you are doing.

Because the root chakra is grounding energy and security, it is time to take back your sexuality, sizzle, and sensuality. Women and men, no matter what age, shape, or size, can be attractive, active, sexy, sexually active, sensual, sizzly, feisty, and passionate. You can accomplish this by activating and doing root chakra movement and exercise every day.

This exercise is designed to help move energy through the root chakra. As you are moving energy, visualize yourself coming alive. Allow passion to be renewed. Feel the body tingle with excitement, and feel beautiful, sexy, and sensual. *Caution: You may feel that sexual urge whether you want to or not.*

It is important to allow fresh energy and ideas in and move old ideas out of this area. Feel a renewed sensuality happening. Allow yourself to fall in love with your body, no matter what its size or shape. When you criticize your body, no matter how large or small, or yourself, you send a message to your soul that you are flawed. The side effect of this may be shame, embarrassment, anger, failure, and apathy. As a result, you may hide your desires under layers of fat and clothing because of fear of failure. Realize that there are no flaws in your body—just flawed thinking, which affects the body.

Readjust your thinking. As you come to believe your body is beautiful just the way it is, those around you will see your confidence and they too will see your beauty. Wear clothes that are flowing and that make you feel sexy. Show some skin if you must to get started. The skin is the largest organ of the body, and it needs to breathe. Quit hiding. Be willing to let the world see you. The response may surprise you.

In this exercise, you are about to learn to allow the skin to feel everything you are experiencing. If you are embarrassed to do this in a group, do this meditation in private until you feel comfortable doing it with others. Build that confidence; build that passion. You are unshakable.

Realize that some may love the newfound freedom; some may hate it. It really doesn't matter as long as you are in love with yourself. When you love yourself, you will automatically draw others to your light. That light of love will make it difficult for others to dislike you. Those who might have trouble with it are probably in the throes of their own self-loathing. But you will recognize their self-loathing state and realize that it has nothing to do with you. You will not take it personally. It is none of your business what others think of you because you can't control it anyway. You will not take on their limitations.

To begin this exercise, stand up straight, stretch the arms up toward the sky, and take in a deep breath through the nose, all the way down to your toes. Hold it a minute, and then release through the mouth with a sigh of AAAAHHHHHH. The "AH" breath is a breath used in the tantric sex exercises to activate and open the root chakra. The breath also allows the chakras to open, and it actually pushes energy into the root chakra. If you must, push down on the lower body as if you are having a bowel movement. Push the plug from the pelvic area, and feel the energy filling up the root chakra. Let it open and activate. Allow the root chakra to begin pulsating in rhythm with your breathing. Focus all your attention on your genital area, feel the tingle, and come alive.

After you have done the breath exercise three times, stand up even taller. Visualize the body anchored to the floor, hips directly over the knees. Now, take a deep breath, and in a deep voice, allow the sound "OH" to escape the throat. Hold the tone as long as you can, and then breathe in and exhale again, with the same tone—"OH." Repeat this three times. Visualize your body, strong in stance, grounded and secure in the conviction of what is right for you. This is the foundation of your belief system. Feel your core beliefs come to the surface to be acknowledged and executed. "You are power, you are grace, you are ALIVE!"

Next, put on some music with a heartbeat momentum. A good choice is, "I Will Survive" by Gloria Gaynor or "YMCA" by the Village People. Make sure the music is upbeat and has a distinctive beating tone, like the heartbeat of the soul. You want your body to feel the rhythmic beat moving through it.

Stand up straight, relax the body, and start swaying the hips from side to side. Gently at first, right to left. Then, as you feel a graceful natural rhythm starting to take hold, move the hips side to side a little faster. By this time, your shoulders should be wanting to join the fun. So, as the hips sway from side to side, dip one shoulder forward in a sexy movement, pull it back, and do the other shoulder. Go ahead and double-time the hips if you have a steady rhythm going. Let your body have a mind of its own, moving and swaying to the music. Allow uncontrolled movements. Dance as if no one is watching! Be silly, be loose, and feel ALIVE!

Once you feel comfortable with the beat and the hips have loosened up, start circling the hips slowly in a clockwise motion. After a while, reverse and make small circles at first. When this feels comfortable, begin to take the hips to the left, front, right, and back in a large, swinging circle. Go slowly at first so you do not hurt yourself. Only do what you can; work your way to more movement as you get more experience. This movement pattern opens up the hip area, and the root chakra can begin to breathe. Go slow and enjoy the ride.

When you feel comfortable with this move, take the rib cage and lift it up toward the chin while engaging your abdominal muscles. Move the rib cage side to side several times. Once your rib cage feels loosened up, push the abdominal muscles out, and roll the muscles of the belly forward, allowing the rib cage to drop. Repeat and continue this motion several times until you get the rhythm of it. It is similar to a belly-dancing move. This movement moves energy through the spleen chakra and solar plexus chakra as well as builds the muscles of the abdomen. When you feel that you have accomplished this move and are comfortable with it, reverse the steps in a backward motion.

Alternate this move with the circular hip and shoulder movements, and really let yourself go to the beat of the music. Jump up and down, dance, get crazy. Have fun. Don't hurt yourself—take it slow at first if you are out of shape.

Keep the beat of the music with the hips and the shoulders, and allow the feet and ankles to sway as well. Bob your head in time with the music; however, be kind to your neck.

By this time, all the parts of the body should be moving in somewhat perfect harmony with each other. If they are not, keep the rhythm of the body moving, and practice the swaying motion of the body. Close your eyes and feel the music. It is a natural move and the more you do it, the more natural it will begin to feel. This swaying motion is activating the root chakra, supplying energy to the rest of the chakras of the body. Do this through the entire length of a song, perhaps three to five minutes.

When you are finished dancing, take another deep breath and release with an "AH" breath. Do this three times, and notice whether you have a refreshed, tingly feeling throughout the body. The hands will buzz. If so, you have opened your root chakra. If you do not feel refreshed and tingly, keep dancing and breathing.

The root chakra will open up whether you want it to or not. You may also see an increase in your sex drive or your desire to look and be sexy. Pounds begin falling off your body, and muscle tone is defined. Your mind may start filling with all sorts of ideas that you would like to accomplish and a sudden desire or passion to implement these ideas. Expect it to happen; let it happen. It is God's will that you be successful, beautiful, healthy, and happy. Take one more "AH" breath, and plant that thought in your subconscious mind.

Now, to balance the rest of the body, sit on the floor or in a comfortable chair and hold a journal and pen. Close your eyes and listen to the silence. Pay attention to what thoughts arise for you. After a few moments of silence, open your eyes and make a note of your thoughts in your journal. Your journal will become your Bible. Read it every day. Write in it every day. These are your quantum mind thoughts of action. Take your journal wherever you go, so when you have a brain splash you can write it down. You may also put on meditation music or a guided meditation to get in touch with the inner quantum mind.

Second Chakra—Spleen Chakra

Sexual and Family Balance

The spleen chakra is located just below the navel. It encompasses the abdomen, lower back, bladder, kidneys, adrenals, lower stomach and pelvic area, and reproductive organs. It is governed by water and is related to emotions and sexuality. The abdominal area houses expressed or repressed emotions from childhood and family issues. The spleen chakra holds childhood and DNA programming and our developed belief system. This controls our will and the ability to interact with others. Use the chakra to do the work on breaking family abuse, programming, and habits and to establish new ones.

The spleen chakra, like the root chakra, is a place of pleasure, intimacy, and intuition. When in balance, the spleen chakra exhibits a healthy family life, a healthy sex life, and the ability to experience pleasure. Emotional reasoning and intellect are intact. A balanced spleen chakra has healthy boundaries and is graceful in movement. When the energy is balanced, one is friendly, outgoing, concerned about others, and gracious.

Lack of energy in the spleen chakra may cause one to be shy, timid, or sexually repressed. Guilt, shame, and blame hide within a weakened spleen chakra. An unstable spleen chakra can be easily manipulated and emotionally blackmailed. Boundaries need to be reset. Repressed childhood memories and religious upbringing or moral severity will gather in this area, causing the lower belly area to distend. A tired spleen chakra will manifest self-criticism and self-loathing.

A traumatized spleen chakra will hold the memories of sexual, emotional, and physical abuse. Sexual issues from too little spleen chakra energy may result in frigidity, impotence, emotional numbness, and fear of pleasure and intimacy. Too much energy stored in the spleen chakra may cause an overabundance of sexual energy or an emotionally charged or explosive personality. It may also cause one to be delusional and obsessed. Addictions could be the outcome of such behavior.

Bladder and kidney problems, childbirth difficulties, pelvis and lower back pain, gynecology problems, and abortions are all associated with a wounded spleen chakra.

The spleen chakra relates to the journey or career (north), family (east), and intimacy (southwest) sectors of the ba gua. Work in these sectors to help explain emotional or sexual issues in your life. The spleen chakra is dependent on the earth element for grounding and containment.

The family sector of the east or intimacy sector of the southwest may help solve issues of family and relationships as well as self-love and sexual and trust issues. Use these areas in conjunction with placed spiritual deities to call in help from the cosmos or God. Facilitate your work by reading the section in this book about the "Ba Gua Sectors."

The spleen chakra is ruled by the color orange. You may also use green and pink to facilitate energy in the spleen chakra. Green and pink can be used to bring in unconditional love for self from God. Metal is needed to boost the energy of the spleen to maintain the healthy ideas associated with family and self.

To begin chakra work, sit down in the north, east, or southwest of your home, depending upon what topics you are working on. Use this area to help release old DNA programming and download new programming to achieve your highest dreams. The north is best for determining new life goals.

Prepare yourself with the mudra. Recite the sound associated with the spleen chakra, and then recite the affirmation. You may use the stones or oils also associated with the chakra to enhance energy. Focus all your attention upon the topic you wish to explore. When you are finished, be sure to journal and log your progress. If you do not, you will forget the messages that came up for you.

Mudra for the spleen chakra for releasing guilt, shame, and resentment. Helps to rejuvenate the energy of the negative past experiences and past conditioning.

With elbows out to your side, place your hands, palms up, in front of the navel area, with the right hand resting in the left hand. Think of a situation you wish to release. Breathe long, deep, slow breaths and release while reciting the spleen chakra mantra—"OOO" (as in pool). Visualize all pent-up feelings releasing from the root, spleen, and solar plexus chakras with each exhale. Replace these feelings with unconditional love, compassion, and understanding for self.

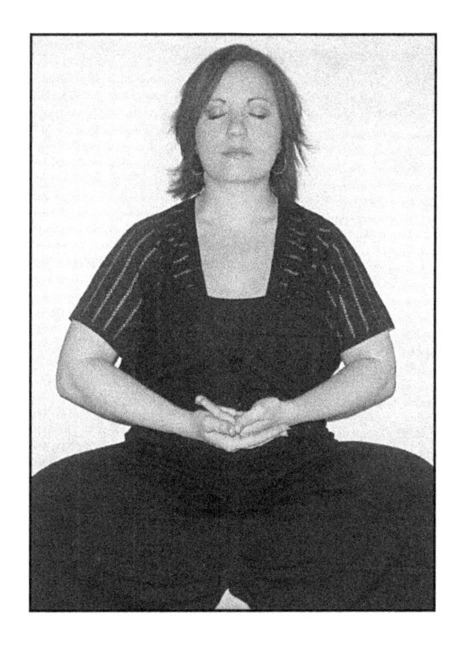

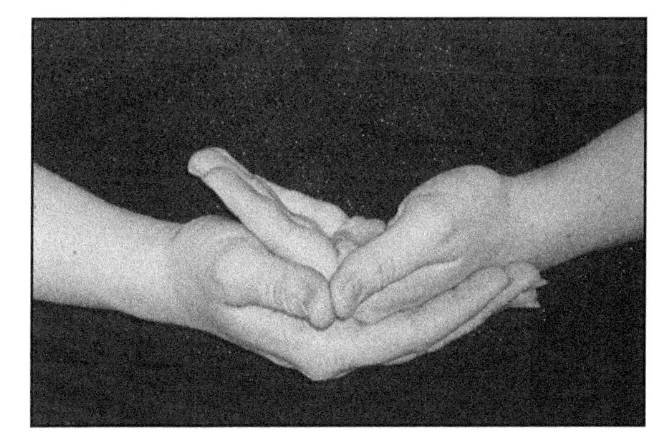

Secondary mudra for the spleen chakra. Used for activating the hormones and adrenals to cleanse your aura and regenerate your cells. Visualize new programming on youth and vitality entering your body:

Sit on the floor with your back straight. Rest your hands on your legs. Make a circle with your thumb and index finger. Stretch the other fingers out straight. Breathe in through the mouth, a short breath with a fast breath exhalation, focusing on the navel. Do this nine times then recite the sound associated with the spleen chakra—"OOO," as in the word *pool*. Do this rhythm for two to three minutes. Alternate breath and sound.

Affirmation for the spleen chakra

"I forgive myself and others. I am grateful for my experiences. I am love, I am beautiful, I am power, I am peace."

Essential oils for the spleen chakra

Geranium: Helps release negative energies, balance the emotions, and lift the spirit; fosters hope and peace.

Grapefruit and/or Orange: Clearing and uplifting; helps unwind and relax; provides a youthful influence.

Sandalwood: Helps remove negative programming.

Pine: Soothes stress and revitalizes the whole body.

Bergamot: Relieves anxiety and decreases anger.

Rose: Intoxicating and aphrodisiac-like; brings balance, harmony, and feelings of love.

Ylang-Ylang: Influences sexual energy and enhances relationships.

Clary Sage: Relaxes and produces dreamlike state; aphrodisiac.

Note: If you are pregnant or nursing, taking medication, or under a doctor's care, be sure to discuss the oils' interactions with the doctor.

Stones that support the spleen chakra

Carnelian: Increases energy.

Amber, Topaz, Citrine: Helps control overwhelming stresses.

Green and Yellow Calcite: Helps dissolve negativity and betrayal.

Rodanite: Promotes self-esteem, self-worth, and self-confidence; aids in restoring physical energy that emotional trauma has dissipated.

Pink Tourmaline: Stimulates love and new friends.

Rose Quartz: Manifests unconditional love for yourself and others; increases self-esteem and attracts loving relationships into our lives; touted by the Egyptians for weight loss and as a wrinkle cure.

Pearl: Stimulates femininity and self-acceptance.

Spleen chakra strengthening exercise

Stand up tall as you did in the spleen chakra exercise. Take a deep breath and let it out to the tone of "OO," as in the word *pool*. The "OO" is the feel-good sound of sexual origin. Hold the tone as long as you can, and then take another deep breath and repeat. Do this three times or more until you can hold the sound effectively. The shorter your ability to hold the sound, the more blocked the chakra. Do this exercise until the sound can be held constant and the body feels a vibration within the abdominal area.

Do this exercise immediately after you do the root chakra sounds. We will progressively move from the root chakra to the throat chakra in a constant moving vibration.

Also do the exercises of the root chakra to strengthen the spleen chakra. Dance, move the hips, make love, laugh, learn to play, and let creativity come to the surface. If your moods are severely out of balance, get your adrenal glands and hormones tested.

Third Chakra—Solar Plexus Chakra

Fire in the Belly
Personal Power and Ego

The solar plexus chakra is located in the diaphragm area, just above the belly button, and it is the power center of the body. The belly button is where our nourishment of life came in when we were in the womb, and that area remains the life force of our being. Our ego is located in the solar plexus chakra. The solar plexus chakra rules our willpower, self-esteem, and self-confidence, thus attracting to us all we desire. The solar plexus is responsible for our ability to act upon a situation and achieve the results intended.

The solar plexus chakra controls our stomach, small intestines, liver, gallbladder, pancreas, spleen, and middle spine. Our metabolism and our ability to digest life resides in this chakra. Health issues arising from unresolved solar plexus issues may be arthritis, ulcers, digestion problems, liver dysfunction, diabetes, and colon problems.

When the solar plexus is in perfect timing with the other chakras, there is a balanced sense of self, not too serious and not too laid back. A balanced ego is capable of making good decisions and is able to meet challenges easily, overcoming all obstacles. When the solar plexus becomes too tired or challenged, a tendency toward frustration, anger, and nervousness may occur. Jealousy, worry, confusion, indigestion, and insecurity creep slowly into your life when you are not expecting it.

An overactive solar plexus may result in bullying of others, explosive behavior, gossip, and manipulation to get one's way. The manipulator will play a victim while acting like a martyr for his or her sacrifices, making him very powerful. He or she gets the attention sought.

An underactive solar plexus may result in one being easily manipulated by others and in a fear of punishment by those in authority. The solar plexus will hold the shame and criticism of childhood. These people usually are seeking approval at any cost.

The solar plexus chakra is ruled by fire and is supported by the abundance or southeast sector of the ba gua, which is ruled by wood, water, and air. The abundance sector of the ba gua attracts to us those things in abundance, such as wealth, health, happiness, family, and friends. Wood generates fire, therefore enhancing the third chakra. The abundance or southeast sector of the home is a great place to work on shifting the paradigms in your life.

Yellow is the color associated with the solar plexus chakra. Purple and green can also be used in solar plexus work for creativity and growth.

To begin chakra work, sit down in the southeast of your home. Use this area to manifest those things in your life that you desire. Be clear and precise. Do not waiver.

Prepare yourself with the mudra. Recite the sound associated with the solar plexus chakra, and then recite the affirmation. You may use the stones or oils also associated with the chakra to enhance energy. Focus all your attention upon the topic you wish to explore. When you are finished, be sure to journal and log your progress. If you do not, you will forget the messages that came up for you.

Mudra for the solar plexus

Bend your elbows and place your hands in front of your body, palms down, with your fingers together and your thumbs hiding in the palms. Make sure your hands are touching at the little fingers. When your hands are facing downward, visualize all negativity flowing from the body into the earth where it can be dispersed and healed. This position is used to release all blockages that stand in the way for receiving the prosperity of health, wealth, and happiness. Breathe long, deep breaths when visualizing release.

Next, turn the hands upward to the heavens and visualize all gifts of the health, wealth, and happiness that God has to offer flowing into your hands and into your body.

Breathe short, fast breaths with each turn. Then breathe long deep breaths while visualizing gifts. Repeat the sound associated with the solar plexus chakra—"AH" as in father.

Do this for a few minutes until you feel that all the blockages have been released and that the body is easily accepting the prosperity.

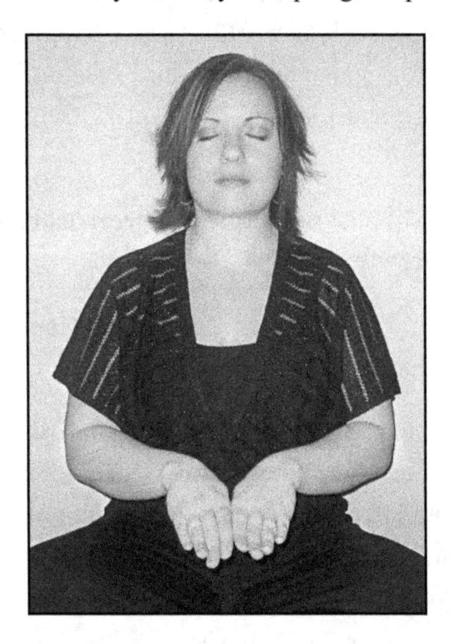

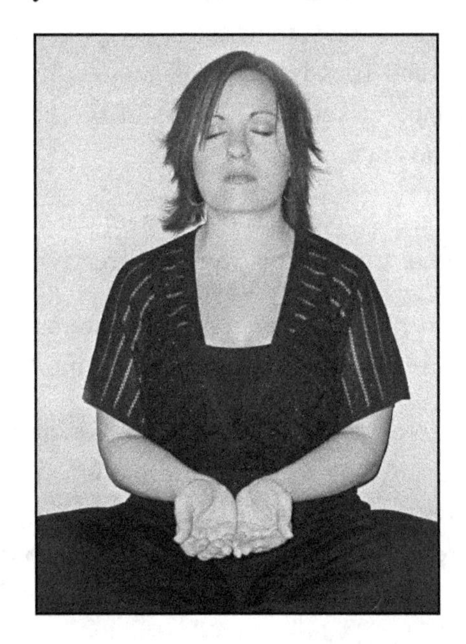

Start with hands down and then turn then up and breathe "AH" or "HAA" or "HAR," meaning *God*.

Affirmation for the solar plexus

"I know what is right for me. I am brave, intelligent, and confident. I am in control of my destiny."

Essential oils for the solar plexus chakra

Frankincense: Used to increase spiritual awareness, strengthen well-being, and promote positive attitude. In ancient times, only those with great wealth possessed such an oil.

Myrrh: Promotes spiritual awareness and is psychologically uplifting. According to legends of the queens, myrrh possesses a frequency of wealth and was a trade commodity.

Cinnamon: Considered the "oil of wealth" from the Orient and part of the formula the Lord gave to Moses (Exodus 30:22–27). It is considered an anti-viral, a purifier, and an oxygenator. Traditionally, cinnamon was thought to have a frequency that attracted wealth and abundance.

Orange, Lemon, or Citrus: Promotes well-being. Helps with clarity of thought. Brings joy, peace, and happiness to those who possess it.

Ginger: Stimulates physical energy, courage, and willpower.

Basil: Helps with mental fatigue.

Note: If you are pregnant or nursing, taking medication, or under a doctor's care, be sure to discuss the oils' interactions with the doctor.

Stones that support the solar plexus chakra

Citrine: Attracts riches and self-empowerment.

Malachite: Clears the path for obtaining a goal; brings inner peace.

Cinnabar: Used to attract abundance.

Sapphire: Used to make our dreams come true.

Topaz: Used to calm our emotions, relieve tension, and restore physical energy.

Amber: Used to help us become more aware of our body's needs, thus promoting better health.

Aventurine: Amplifies leadership qualities, and helps us to attain our goals.

Exercise to release nervousness

According to the book *Bushido, The Way of the Samurai*, the Samurai were taught to avoid nervousness by applying spit to their earlobes and breathing deeply through both nostrils. It was also recommended they go outside and kick everything in their path to release any other pent-up energy. In today's society, we can exercise, break glass, throw things—whatever it takes to expel that excess nervous energy. When pent-up energy is released, apply the spit and breathe.

For nervousness caused by indecision, walk away, apply spit to your earlobes, and give yourself more time to think about it. Bring yourself to a place of power by saying, "I need to think about it more." The indecision is there for a reason: honor it. Discuss any hesitations you may have with a trusted friend. Make clear agreements. Confront the matter head on. Never turn your back to the enemy. It makes you vulnerable.

Chakra-balancing meditation to enhance personal power

To balance this chakra, do deep-breathing exercises by breathing in through the nose and out through the mouth, exhaling all the air from the lungs. As you breathe in, put your tongue behind your front teeth on the roof of your mouth, as you exhale, relax the tongue. Visualize the stress leaving the body on the exhale. If you need to, rub your stomach in a clockwise motion to expel any pent-up emotions. Do this three times. After you get the breathing down comfortably, start visualizing the energy moving from the solar plexus chakra ("AH"), down to the spleen chakra ("OO"), on down to the root chakra ("OH"). Now reverse and come back up to the spleen chakra ("OO") and then to the solar plexus chakra ("AH"), pausing at each chakra and really feeling the energy each offers. At this point, you should feel grounded.

Next, take the energy from the solar plexus chakra up the body to the heart chakra located in the middle of the chest and say the mantra "AY," then to the throat chakra and say the mantra "EE." Pause at each chakra. Next comes the third eye chakra located in the middle of the forehead. The sound associated with the third eye chakra is the traditional "OHM." From the third eye chakra, move to the top of the head, known as the crown chakra. Pause for a brief moment of silence. Now, with sound and pausing at each chakra along the way, bring the energy back to the solar plexus chakra. When you reach the solar plexus chakra, take three deep breaths again, breathing in through your nose and out through your mouth with the "AH" breath.

When you are finished, sit quietly and meditate. Focus on your body's strength. See what concerns may arise. Do this every day until you can move the energy comfortably. Be sure to journal at the end of each meditation.

Fourth Chakra—Heart Chakra

Giving and Receiving

The heart chakra is located in the middle of the chest, just above the heart. It is the center of compassion, love, and peace. The heart chakra is governed by fire and is associated with the health center of the ba gua. The heart chakra is the center of all the chakras, as is the health center, the center of the ba gua. The heart chakra is the center of the healing energies. The information travels downward from the crown chakra to the heart chakra and upwards from the root chakra. It meets at the heart chakra in complete harmony with our desires—hence the phrase "the heart's desire."

The heart chakra is associated with heart and circulatory system, lungs, shoulder and arms, ribs, breasts, and thymus gland. A weakened heart chakra may present as heart issues such as heart attack, high cholesterol, high blood pressure; lung issues such as asthma/allergy, bronchitis, pneumonia, emphysema, or cancer; upper back/shoulder problems; or breast problems.

The heart chakra controls our ability to love and be loved. It opens us up to new experiences and relationships. When this chakra is balanced, we are loving, giving, compassionate, understanding, and in touch with our feelings and the feelings of others. The immune system is healthy and the mind at peace. A balanced heart chakra works to make the world a better place. We feel others' pain.

An imbalanced heart chakra holds nurturing issues. Betrayal, unacknowledged grief and hurt, rejection, abandonment, and anger lie within the hurt heart chakra. Jealousy, insecurities, and codependency may make love demanding and controlling. One might even enjoy others' pain.

People whose heart chakra is out of balance will tend to feel sorry for themselves and think the world is all about them—the "woe is me" martyr/victim effect. This lack of energy in the heart chakra may cause paranoia and a belief that everyone is against them. This can manifest in a weakened immune system.

People are the reflection of who they are. If someone cannot give love, he or she cannot receive it and return it back to the world. This deficient energy will tend to search out its own kind. They will find relationships that do not fulfill them based upon their inability to trust and love unconditionally. Drama and pain are equated with love. Remember the old adage, "misery loves company."

To bring the heart chakra back into balance, give freely of yourself to a service-oriented project. Perhaps volunteer at the hospital or hospice. As you become acquainted with others in need, you tend to forget your own problems.

Learn to cry freely. Watch sad movies to get the emotion in the heart spinning again. Play with children, get happy, and laugh with them. Give everyone you meet a hug, even if it is a struggle at first. You will find it easier to do with each hug. Most importantly, though, learn to love yourself. Realize that from this moment forward you are in charge of your destiny. Make the decision to love and forgive yourself for not being perfect. If you were perfect, you would be God.

The colors of green for healing and pink for love give energy to the fire of the heart chakra.

To begin the heart chakra work, sit down in the center of your home. Use this area to enhance feelings of love and to clear past resentments and hurt. Prepare yourself with the mudra. Recite the sound associated with the heart chakra, and then recite the affirmation. You may use the stones or oils also associated with the chakra to enhance energy.

Focus all your attention upon the topic you wish to explore. When you are in the middle of grief or heartbreak, it is important to understand the larger issue—the reason it is happening. This mudra will help relax and heal the heart as well as the nerves.

When you are finished, be sure to journal and log your progress. If you do not, you will forget the messages that came up for you.

Mudra for the heart chakra

Place your hands together at the heart center of the body. Breathe long, slow breaths, and feel the energy coming in the top of your head, into your heart, and down your arms into the palms of your hands. Visualize a circle of love from your heart to the arms to the hands and back again—all the time visualizing the color pink or green. This mudra from the heavens is giving and receiving energy to the body. Recite the sound associated with the heart chakra—"AY."

Affirmation for the heart chakra

"I will love and serve, and be loved and be served."

Essential oils for the heart chakra

Rose: Brings in peace, harmony, and love.

Clove: Lifts depression and increases energy.

Patchouli: Calms and relaxes; helps with grounding.

Sandalwood: Brings healing and balance; aids in promoting sleep.

Pine: Soothes mental stress and revitalizes the body.

Note: If you are pregnant or nursing, taking medication, or under a doctor's care, be sure to discuss the oils' interactions with the doctor.

Stones that support the heart chakra

Rose Quartz: Promotes love and emotional well-being.

Emerald: Promotes overall well-being.

Tourmaline: Promotes emotional well-being.

Jade: Promotes and maintains healing of the vital organs.

Green Aventurine: Promotes overall well-being.

Malachite: Promotes overall well-being.

Heart-calming meditation

This meditation calms the physical body, opens the mind, and connects you to the spirit.

Begin with the heart-calming mudra. Place your hands together at the heart center of the body. Breathe long, slow breaths, and feel the energy coming in the top of your head, into your heart, and down your arms into the palms of your hands.

Create an intention of the heart and mind becoming still and calm. Visualize a white light around the body and a glow coming from the heart chakra. Move the energy of your body from the solar plexus chakra to your heart chakra.

Chant the following mantra nine times:

Gate Gate (Got tay Got tay)

Para Gate (Pair-a Got tay)

Para Sam Gate (Pair-a Sum Got tay)

Bodhi Swaha (Bo-dee Swa-ha)

(This mantra means "gone, gone, gone beyond, gone completely beyond enlightenment.")

Allow yourself just to float into the meditative state, and see what may come up to the conscious mind. Write everything down that happens during the meditation, everything that comes into your consciousness. Do this so you may go back and read it again and again until you can make sense of it.

Note: When in the meditative or dreamlike state, you will forget what you experience unless you write it down immediately.

Fifth Chakra—Throat Chakra

Voice to the World

Vibration is the most important part of the throat chakra. The throat chakra is located at the base of the throat and is our communication center to the world. It is used for hearing sounds, speaking words, and for taste and smell. The colors turquoise, lighter blues, or grays are associated with this chakra center. Blue is one of the greatest healing rays when it comes to the chakras. It quiets the body but stimulates the spiritual levels in our mind.

The throat chakra encompasses the throat, ears, nose, sinus, thyroid, trachea, mouth, teeth, tongue, and gums. Afflictions may include issues of the ears, nose, and throat, mouth ulcers, gum difficulties, and thyroid problems.

The throat is related to the creativity sector of the west and the benefactor sector of the northwest. The throat chakra is governed by the element of metal and is related to communication and creativity. This chakra not only controls the way we are able to express ourselves—either through speech, art, or music—but also the way we are able to listen, understand, and communicate with others.

When creativity is low, the psyche becomes low and the ability to communicate becomes suppressed. The benefactor's area can help manifest teachers or friends to inspire us to create and communicate. The throat chakra and the benefactor's area are ruled by the ether—the upper region of space known as Heaven.

When the throat chakra is balanced, there is a good sense of being centered. The communication and artistic abilities become fluid. There is an added sense of divine energy. One will honor his or her word.

Children who were victims of authoritarian parents with the mindset that children are to be seen and not heard will have weak throat chakras. They will hold back from expressing thoughts, beliefs, and fears for worry of looking foolish. Children who were given no rights to speak or who were always ridiculed as wrong will be shy and frightened by public speaking situations. They may also have difficulties getting centered and may experience misunderstandings about their personal spiritual beliefs. They may stutter or lose focus when speaking.

Those with an overactive throat chakra may lie, yell, and abuse. They are quite the opposite of the shy ones. They will boast, exaggerate, and have a tendency toward lying. They will chatter quickly without really having a point of conversation.

To balance this chakra, one should sing, recite poetry, or read Dr. Seuss stories aloud. Also, chant mantras or say "OHM" or hum. Tune into vibrations, such as listening to musical instruments and chimes.

To begin the throat chakra work, sit down in the west or northwest sector of the home. Use this area to find your voice, to express yourself clearly, and develop your creativity. You may use the stones or oils also associated with the chakra to enhance energy. When you are finished, be sure to journal and log your progress. If you do not, you will forget the messages that came up for you.

Mudra for the throat chakra

Sit with a straight spine and your upper arms raised shoulder height, parallel to the ground. Bend your elbows so your hands are at ear level. Close your hands in a fist and extend your thumbs toward your temples. Breathe short, fast breaths through your mouth, bringing energy into your throat. Take three short breaths and relax with one long deep breath. Recite the sound associated with the throat chakra—"EEE," as in the word *sleep*. This mudra will strengthen your ability to focus and speak with your highest integrity. It helps to make correct choices under pressure.

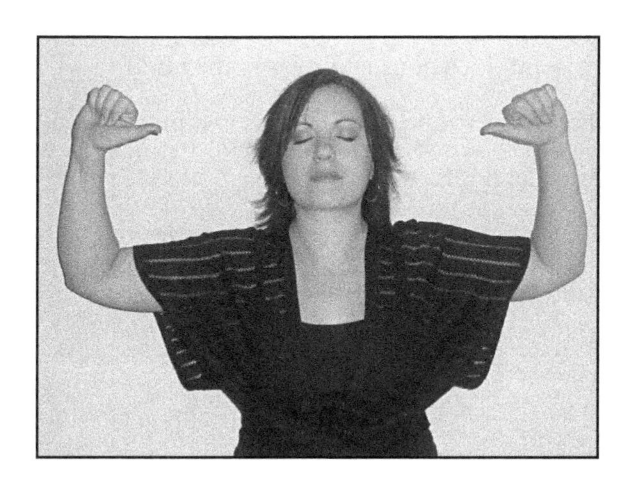

Affirmation for the throat chakra

"I speak with love and tact, expressing myself precisely and creatively."

Essential oils for the throat chakra

Lemongrass: Fragrance promotes psychic awareness and purification.

Lavender: Helps create assistance and acceptance.

Bergamot: Increases creativity, concentration, and mental focus.

Chamomile: Calms and relaxes; may be used to dispel anger, thus stabilizing the emotions.

Frankincense: Promotes spiritual awareness and meditation.

Hyssop: Stimulates creativity and meditation.

Note: If you are pregnant or nursing, taking medication, or under a doctor's care, be sure to discuss the oils' interactions with the doctor.

Stones that support the throat chakra

Turquoise: Eases mental tensions and relaxes the mind.

Blue Topaz: Relieves stress and tension; aids communication.

Aquamarine: Calms and relaxes.

Emerald: Promotes creativity and perception; relaxes the body.

Red Coral: Strengthens the voice.

Crystal Quartz: Increases clear communication.

Meditation for the throat chakra

Close your eyes, and start the breathing exercises by breathing in through the nose with the tongue on the roof of the mouth behind the front teeth and then letting out the breath, relaxing the tongue on the exhales. Do this three times, then begin breathing normally. Listen to all the sounds around you. Pay attention to any vibratory sound you may hear. When you feel comfortable and centered, recite the mantra "Ohm Ma Ne Pad Me Hum." Do this very slowly, and let each sound resonate the appropriate chakra, starting at the root chakra and moving sound to the crown chakra. Feel the vibrations resonating and balancing each chakra. Visualize each chakra spinning in a clockwise direction.

Feel the throat chakra opening up to perfect speech and expression. Visualize a blue glowing light coming from the throat chakra. Know that this light is the perfect expression of your soul. From this moment forward, your ability to articulate your thoughts into words will be made in a perfectly natural way. Each day, you will speak clearly and enunciate your words with more confidence than you ever thought possible. And if that is okay with you, just continue breathing normally. Take a few moments and pay attention to your thoughts; when you are ready, allow your eyes to open.

Sixth Chakra—Third Eye Chakra

Intuition and Knowing

The third eye chakra is located in the middle of the forehead, just above the eyes. The third eye chakra is the center of our psychic powers or intuition. It is the guide to the higher self. In this center, we experience extrasensory perception, channeling, and past life memories. It is our path to "seeing," both physically and intuitively.

The third eye chakra is governed by metal and relates to the self-knowledge area of the northeast and the benefactor's area of the northwest of the ba gua. The third eye relates to getting to know more about yourself and your higher power of the mind. It houses your dreams, imagination, and visions. The colors violet or indigo blue are associated with the third eye chakra.

The third eye relates to brain, eyes, nervous system, pineal gland, and the pituitary gland. It may relate to the ears and nose as well. Afflictions associated with the third eye chakra are vision disturbances, blindness/deafness, headaches, delusional behavior, nightmares, brain tumor/hemorrhage/stroke, seizures, and learning disabilities. Mood swings, anxiety, and depression may also be associated with the third eye chakra and the pineal gland.

When this chakra is in balance, you receive daily spiritual guidance and have no fear of death. You are the master of self. There is no need for validation outside of self. Intuition and perception are good.

Too much mental energy in this chakra can make you egotistical, religiously aggressive, and manipulative. Confusion sets in, and God-like behavior emerges.

Too little energy in this chakra may cause you to feel lost and to search for validation outside of self. You become afraid of success and are undisciplined and timid. Mental illness can be associated with this chakra imbalance. A person with too little energy in this chakra may lack clarity and psychic energy.

Sit down in the northeast–self-knowledge or northwest–benefactor's sector of the home, and use this area to develop your connection to your higher power and to develop your intuition. To balance this chakra, meditate often, and visualize a violet fire coursing through your veins, bringing directive thought into reality. You may use the stones or oils associated with the chakra to enhance energy. When you are finished, be sure to journal and log your progress. If you do not, you will forget the messages that came up for you.

Mudra for unlocking the subconscious mind

Place your hands, arms bent, in front of your stomach. Curl your fingers inward to the pads of your hands, thumb tips touching, and the knuckles of the index and middle finger touching. No other fingers should be touching. Point the thumb toward the heart chakra. Breathe long and slow. This mudra will aid in opening the subconscious mind and clearing it of all blockage. Meditate with the sound associated with the third eye chakra—"OHM"—or affirmations. Breathe slow, deep breaths in the nose and out the mouth.

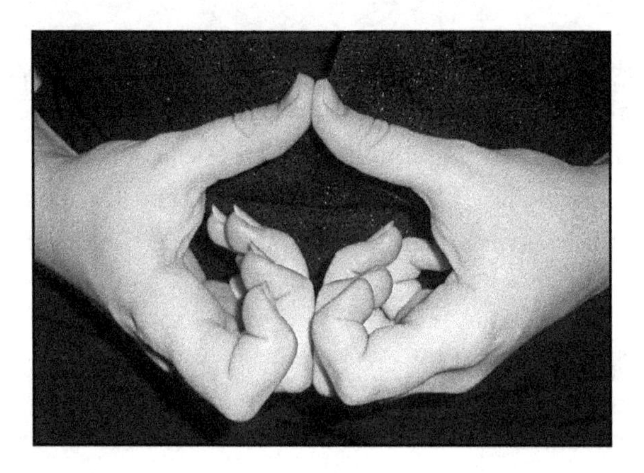

Mudra for projection of perception energy for the third eye chakra

Lift your hands between the stomach and heart area with elbows bent, arms to the side. Touch the middle knuckles of the last three fingers together. Point your index finger and thumb away from the body, and place the pads together. Touch your thumbs to the solar plexus of the body. Breathe deep, slow breaths. This chakra builds trust and self-confidence and adjusts the energy of the perception center. Meditate with the sound associated with the third eye chakra—"OHM"—or affirmation.

Affirmation for third eye chakra

"I invoke the wisdom of the violet flame. I trust my knowing. It flows freely every day, making everything clear and concise. Today, I listen."

Essential oils for the third eye chakra

Juniper: Evokes feelings of health, love, and peace; may elevate spiritual awareness.

Peppermint: Purifies and stimulates the conscious mind.

Birch: Increases, on all levels, the awareness of the senses.

Chamomile: Helps to relax and clear the subconscious mind.

Clary Sage: Produces dreamlike stages.

Note: If you are pregnant or nursing, taking medication, or under a doctor's care, be sure to discuss the oils' interactions with the doctor.

Stones that support the third eye chakra

Lapis Lazuli: Stimulates wisdom and truth.

Quartz Crystal: Elevates thoughts.

Sapphire: The gem of destiny.

Opal: Greek astrologers used this stone to open the mind to visions; used to strengthen mind and the memory.

Amazonite: Used for the pineal gland to inspire faith and hope.

Sodalite: Used to release subconscious fears (when subconscious fears begin to release, be sure to replace the fear with understanding).

Meditation for the third eye chakra

Once you have achieved total relaxation, focus all your attention to the middle of the forehead, also known as the third eye chakra. This area holds the secrets of directive power over our abilities. The third eye contains our higher self and all-knowing clairvoyant records. In most people, the third eye is closed and becomes active when attention is directed to it. In this process, focus your attention to the middle of the forehead, with closed eyes, as if looking at it with your two eyes. As you give attention to your third eye, feel the pulsating energy begin building. Notice how the forehead begins to open and feel alive. Vital energy, gathering in this area, pulses with anticipation. Feel yourself taking a quantum leap into full conscious awareness, a quantum leap from one energy state into another. As you become still and connected, you feel the THIRD EYE OPEN. Your quantum mind has become activated and is ready to receive the wisdom of the violet flame.

The violet flame is a fire that burns deep within the spirit of man—a fire of passion used to turn creative thought into materialized reality. This violet fire lies between the subconscious mind and its link to the cosmos. It is the flame of passion, it is the flame of desire, it is the flame of power—and that is why the wisdom of the violet flame is activated only by those who understand its use. It is the ability to transmute creative thought from the source of divinity into physical, materialized reality through the secret of the senses of the human body.

Imagine now in your mind's eye, behind the third eye, a purplish blue flame that resembles a pilot light on a stove. Continue to relax totally, mind and body, not moving, not even moving a muscle. Focus only on your breath; feel the body in rhythmic harmony with the mind and spirit as you feel the pilot to the violet flame ignite. Allow this flame to grow larger and larger, moving cosmic energy and knowing throughout the entire body. As you breathe, the flame moves through the body, opening all channels of your energy centers, dissolving what needs dissolved and activating all that needs enhanced.

You feel as though your body is floating as it fills with a vital energy, an internal vibration. As you are moving your thoughts forward, you find that your awareness is also moving. You feel as though there are no questions in the world, only answers. You feel as though peace of mind and destiny are accepted without hesitation, as it is the will of the universe. YOU ARE YOUR OWN MASTER, connected to the source of divinity in a way you never thought possible. Continue to see and feel the violet fire course through your veins, and when you are ready, simply open your eyes and be fully conscious and aware with a new knowing of your destiny.

Seventh Chakra—Crown Chakra

God Consciousness

The crown chakra is located on the top of the head. The crown chakra is gold or white in color, and it relates to pure awareness in our consciousness—Christ consciousness. It is our connection to the higher power of our God. It is all-knowing. This chakra brings in wisdom, peace, understanding, spiritual guidance, and universal love for all. The crown chakra is associated with the fame sector of the home.

The fame sector controls our destiny in this world. Destiny is who we are and what we are, according to our divine path. In our lifetime, we wander in and out of our destiny, but something (higher self) always seems to guide us back. This sector is governed by fire, which, when used in reference to the crown chakra, could be called "cosmic energy."

The crown chakra relates to the brain and all of its functions, as well as the skin and the muscular and skeletal systems of the body. When this chakra is in alignment, we have total access to the conscious and subconscious mind. We transcend the laws of nature. Hope and faith abound.

However, when this chakra is out of balance or is partially active, there is no joy and instead one experiences a sense of loss and untapped power. Frustration and depression can run high. Energetic disorders such as sensitivity to light and sound, ADD, learning disabilities, and other environmental factors are signs the crown chakra is clouded and questioning.

When the crown chakra is clouded, there is a violation between your core belief system and your spiritual belief system. Perceptions you received as a child through programming may not be in keeping with the spiritual energetic pattern of your divine path.

To bring this chakra back into balance, meditate, meditate, meditate in the northwest or northeast sector of the home. Surround yourself in peace. Find quiet time and think. As the crown chakra activates and fully opens, you may experience vision changes, hearing changes, and headaches.

Lotus mudra associated with crown chakra

On each hand, place your thumb and little finger together. Place your ring fingers back to back together. Interlock the remaining fingers, right hand under left. This mudra is used as a universal symbol of peace and harmony and of the crown chakra's opening to all possibilities of the universe. Use the sound associated with the crown chakra—"OHM"—or just be silent.

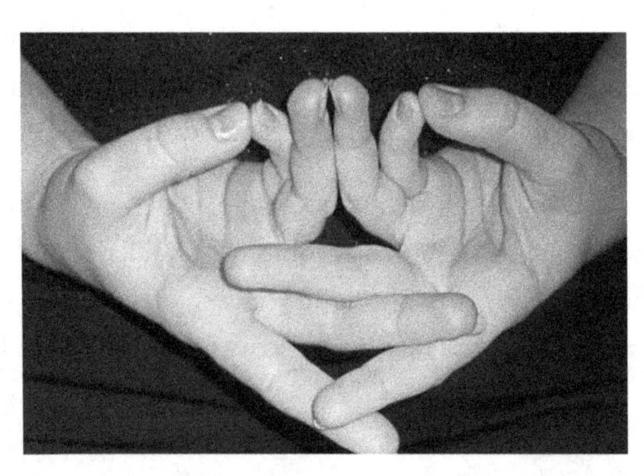

Affirmation for the crown chakra

"I Am who I am in all its mystery."

"I Am protected by the white light of Christ through which no negativity can penetrate."

Essential oils for the crown chakra

Cedarwood: Used to calm and purify; used as incense and for medicinal purposes in Tibet.

Canadian Red Cedar: Traditionally used by Native Americans to enter a "higher realm."

Atlas Cedar: Promotes spirituality.

Nelori: Ancient Egyptians used this oil for its properties of healing the mind, body, and spirit.

Note: If you are pregnant or nursing, taking medication, or under a doctor's care, be sure to discuss the oils' interactions with the doctor.

Stones that support the crown chakra

Amethyst: Increases our natural intuition and helps us get in touch with our inner self.

Diamond: The most powerful stone of all; absorbs all energies, positive and negative. When directed by light and thought, the diamond promotes an inner sense of power and well-being.

Fluorite: Abolishes impediments to spiritual growth.

Black Tourmaline: Has high electric and magnetic properties that attract these energies; absorbs negative energy, entering the home through the earth or electromagnetic devices; also absorbs negative energy radiated from the computer.

Note: Stones should be cleaned periodically when used to absorb negative energies. They may be cleaned by placing in the moonlight or the rain for up to a day. Or you may pass them through a smudge of sage, sweet grass, or frankincense. You may also place them under hot and cold running water for up to five minutes. A final option is to use one tablespoon of sea salt in a cup of spring water and soak overnight.

This chakra completes the three realms of influence: heaven, earth, and human. If we were to lie down in the doorway of your home, your root chakra is on the doorstep. This is the foundation of your being, signifying earth. Your heart or heart chakra is in the middle of the ba gua, or the home, signifying human. Your head or crown chakra is in the sitting position of the ba gua, signifying heaven, thus completing the home and the three realms of influence. You can look to the influences of the home for the grounding or spiritual area of this influence.

The two minor chakras in the hands and the feet are important in healing and meditation. As you move energy through your body into your hands and feet, there should be a throbbing at the chakra points. This is energy crossing the vortex of the energy center, either bringing energy into the body or letting the energy release from the body. Do this simple meditation to direct energy now to these minor chakra centers.

Begin by closing your eyes. As you stand up straight, bring your arms up in the air, perpendicular to the body. Take a deep breath and focus all your attention on your heart chakra in the middle of your chest. Feel the energy travel from your heart chakra, down your arms, and into your hands. Focus, and feel the palms of your hands start to pulsate. Feel the directive power of the mind as it moves energy into your left hand. The temperature of your hand starts to rise, and your palm start to pulsate. Open your eyes and look at your hands—notice the redness. As energy is directed to the hands, the hands will look mottled. Close your eyes again.

Now bring that energy of your left hand back up your arm, through your heart chakra, and move the energy down your right arm and into your right hand. Feel the energy as it travels. As you focus all your energy on your right hand, the temperature of the hand begins to rise and pulsate. Open your eyes and look at the hand. Is it mottled or speckled? Take a deep breath. Repeat process for the left arm and hand. Practice this directive power to hands at least once a day. Use this energy in your hands to feel the energy or auras of objects or people in your environment.

You may also use this directive power to your feet as you are doing a releasing meditation. Do the same meditation as above, beginning at the root chakra, traveling energy down the leg and into the right leg, and then repeat the process for the left leg. Do the right side first, as it is the yang side—or stronger side—of the body and mind. Always remember to take cleansing breaths.

Part FIVE

Self-Hypnosis/Meditation Techniques

Manifesting Your Highest Potential

Meditation, self-hypnosis, guided imagery, and prayer are all words that mean the same thing but are executed in different ways, groups, and meanings.

Meditation or self-hypnosis is a relaxed state of being in which the conscious mind relaxes and the subconscious mind is allowed to come forward and receive new information about life and its purpose. During this process, we are also faced with making new decisions about old behavior patterns. The subconscious mind is the computer master board where all memories and imagination are housed. We must dump old memories and behaviors before new ones can be manifested. Beliefs such as "I never have any money," "I will never be able to do that, "Good things always happen to other people," "I am depressed all the time," and others must be cracked before our highest potential can be manifested.

I call this emptying your coffee cup. Once your cup is full, new coffee cannot be put in it. Consequently, we are stuck with stale coffee or stale ideas. To attract new ideas, we must empty and clean our cup of all old coffee (behaviors) so new ones can manifest. We don't drink stale coffee, so why stay attached to old stale habits or behaviors that no longer serve us? These behaviors and outlooks need to be changed on a subconscious level before our conscious physical life can change.

To get to the master board, we must get past the "gatekeeper." The gatekeeper is the line between the conscious mind and the subconscious mind. The gatekeeper or belief system is the keeper of our safety. It allows only that information that is in keeping with the standards taught to us in childhood to enter the subconscious mind. The gatekeeper believes this information or programming has kept us secure throughout our lives. Unfortunately, our master board may house a lot of negative programming from childhood, and even adulthood, that may be responsible for our unfulfilled soul and spirit. The conscious mind may not even be aware of this behavior process. The purpose of the self-hypnosis method is to help the conscious mind become aware of unconscious or subconscious activity and make a conscious effort to change it. To make these changes, we must use commitment and tenacity. This journey can be rough, but it's worth it.

During meditation or the self-hypnosis process, it is important to distract the gatekeeper with music or a repetition of affirmations of new decisions and desires. As the gatekeeper becomes confused by the change of speech patterns or distractions, splashes of wisdom creep into the subconscious, piece by piece, making new and more appropriate decisions about our life path. New programming then begins to take place on the master board. When this happens, I tell people, "Confusion is good." The belief system is changing.

Until the subconscious mind finally establishes the new behaviors, the gatekeeper or the belief system must remain confused by affirmations of change. Repetition is the key. It takes twenty-eight continuous days to begin altering a behavior. Once the new affirmations become a new behavior, the conscious mind and subconscious mind then work together in perfect harmony, bringing in messages from the divine or the cosmos. Chains of addictions, weight issues, self-esteem values, motivational problems, stress, and spiritual questions can all be realigned and rebalanced at this time.

As in traditional prayer, we receive this information from powers higher than our individual selves, whether they be the higher self, angels, God, cosmos, Great Spirit, spirit guide, or whatever you wish to call them. We then use this information to make changes within our behavior and our life. What we desire on the conscious level, the subconscious mind will help us manifest. Be clear on those desires. We do not get into a taxicab and tell the driver, "I don't want to go to the airport. I don't want to go the hotel. I don't want to go to the hospital." We tell the taxicab driver where we want to go, and we expect to arrive there. The mind works the same way. Unless we are specific, our mind or spirit has no idea where we want to go or how to get there. Once we tell our mind where we desire to be, we will get there. Be specific. Make a plan. Plant an intention. Change your vibration.

To begin preparing for the meditation process, I would like you to go back to the chapter called "Grounding the Root Chakra" and refresh your memory. Do the exercise on grounding the root chakra to align the root-grounding chakra with the other six floors of chakras. This will allow the third eye chakra or crown chakra to receive the messages more clearly. Without the grounding, the information coming into the third eye chakra or crown chakra may not be as clear.

Do not worry or panic; you cannot do it wrong. We know inherently what to do with such information at the right time when it is needed. However, I would like to stress that we will always have messages coming through that don't make sense at that moment in time. Give it time to unfold before you.

These meditations are designed to help you get in touch with exactly what it is you want to manifest in your life and how to achieve it. If you follow the process involved and stay true to its nature, your goals and aspirations will be revealed to you. Learn to use your awareness skills given to you through sight, smell, touch, feel, hearing, and of course the sixth sense of sensing. Learn to advance the consciousness of the senses.

Since the 1950s, it has been known that a baby's mind responds and develops faster when the baby's eyes are exposed to black-and-white pictures. Here are some pictures of illusion that bring a higher mind forward. Study the following pictures, and allow the eye to take a leap in consciousness to see what is there.

Can you find three faces?

Can you see the old man or two lovers kissing?

Can you find the dog?

Can you see the baby?

Don't always believe what you see. See what you believe.

(Tip your head sideways to the left.)

Concentrate on the four small dots in the middle of the picture for about twenty seconds. Then take a look at a wall near you (any smooth, white surface). You will see a circle of light developing. Start by blinking your eyes a couple of times, and you will see a figure emerging. What do you see? Moreover, whom do you see?

Sometimes you have to see the negative to accentuate the positive.

— Tina Falk, Riverton, Utah

Do you see a sensual couple or eight dolphins?

When children were presented with this picture, they only saw the dolphins or they saw only the woman (mom). This is the reason it is important to understand the frame of reference someone is coming from before we assume anything or make prejudgment calls. Always ask yourself, "What does this mean to me?" Ask your spouse or child, "What does this mean to you?"

Learn to see an aura.

Practice seeing things that are hidden. Study pictures of optical illusions and complete crossword puzzles and picture finds. Keep the mind sharp. By doing this, we develop our eyes, brain, and mental capabilities, and we increase the power of the quantum mind. Soon, we can look at the pictures and see in two visions exactly what is there.

Basic Relaxation Technique

Use this technique before any meditation.

To prepare for this meditation, get comfy in your favorite chair or lie down on your bed. It is important to keep your legs and arms uncrossed. In the meditative state, the limbs may tend to feel very heavy, and they might fall asleep. This meditation may be more effective if completed in the self-knowledge or fame sector of your ba gua. You may wish to use a blanket, as body temperature may lower in the meditative state. You may wish to use the oils or stones associated with the chakra you are wishing to enhance or the ba gua sector in which you are working.

Begin by placing your left hand on your stomach or solar plexus area and your right hand over your heart area. Get comfortable, adjust your body, take a deep breath. If you wish, recite a calming mantra of some kind, such as "Ohm Ma Ne Pad Me Hum," which means "to reach enlightenment" and is easy to learn and remember.

Placing your tongue just behind your front teeth, begin by taking in three deep breaths—breathe in through the nose and breathe out through the mouth, exhaling all the air from the lungs. With each inhale, visualize clear, fresh, pure air entering your body. As you exhale, allow all stresses and anxieties of the day to melt and leave the body easily and naturally. If needed, rub your stomach in a clockwise motion to help dispel any stored-up energy, all the while telling your body to "relax and release."

Now, roll your eyes gently upward, and stare at a spot on the ceiling for a few moments. When your eyes tire, slowly allow them to close. The small muscles around the eyelids are relaxing. You may notice a slight twitch as they relax even deeper. As you are relaxing, you may feel the need to swallow. This is the throat muscles starting to relax and opening up your power of expression, which is housed within the throat chakra. This is the sign that the body is responding and relaxing to the commands of your mind. As the throat chakra relaxes, allow your creative juices to begin flowing and creating all those wishes and dreams your heart desires. Allow this to happen. Expect this to happen. Commit to it and it will happen.

Now, inhale again—hold it—push out your stomach muscles as far as you can, and exhale with a big "AHHHHHH," pushing all the air from the diaphragm. Do this two more times. Inhale, hold the breath, push out the stomach muscles, and exhale with a big "AHHHHHHH." One more time. Inhale, push out the stomach muscles, and release—"AHHHH." Now, continue breathing normally; allow the body just to relax. Focus your awareness on just relaxing.

Start by relaxing your feet. You may wish to wiggle them to get more comfortable. If need be, move and wiggle your entire body to get really comfortable. Allow the relaxation to travel up your legs, into your thighs and hips. Just let the world melt away, and notice as you relax, the profound sensation of the body. Take a deep breath and just permit your whole body to relax even deeper. The relaxation energy continues to travel up your spine, into your neck, and down your arms. Take another deep breath and just allow it to happen. As the relaxation energy travels up your neck and into your head, notice the increased awareness in the senses.

Listen to sounds around you; notice how clear they sound. Smell the fragrances around you. See behind your closed eyes all the visions you see with your eyes open. See the detail of a beautiful day, whether it is the colorful flowers, the blue sky, the green grass, the butterflies, the birds, the animals, or the people. Be aware of how the senses become your guide. Observe the enhanced awareness of your senses.

Notice how powerful and in control you feel—how safe you are.

Let's focus your attention, again, to the whole body. Are there any spots on the body that do not feel relaxed? If there are, move your hand mudra to that area. Tell this area, "It is okay to relax; you are safe." Repeat: "Safe and relaxed, safe and relaxed." Take one more deep breath and expect the whole body to relax totally, knowing that at any time you can respond to an emergency if need be.

Body relaxing, body relaxing, deeper and deeper into your own euphoric trance state, and remembering always, "All is well."

Allow the body just to relax and reflect. When you feel it appropriate, allow the eyes to open and the body to be fully aware, conscious, and at peace with the universe.

Meditation

Attracting Health, Wealth, and Happiness into Your Life

Begin this meditation with the basic relaxation technique in the preceding meditation.

After relaxation is achieved, become aware of every muscle, fiber, and tissue of your body. Now, focus on the solar plexus chakra, just above the navel. The solar plexus chakra is the power center of the body. It gives you the determination to manifest those things in your life that you wish to have.

As you continue to relax deeper and deeper, imagine yourself now sitting in the middle of a green field—green being symbolic of money, nature, healing, or anything else you are wishing to manifest at this time. As you are sitting in the middle of this field, notice how peaceful and content it feels. The grass is lush and full. You are at peace.

As you look around, you discover that the green field is actually a field of green money. See how green and lush the money is. Actually look at it and make an impression in your mind of how it feels to the body to have the money all around you. Describe in your mind what it feels like when you touch the money. Ingrain this impression in your subconscious mind.

Now, smell the money. What smells do you associate with the money? Expensive cigars, fine wines, new car interior, fresh paint, new clothing, whatever. Ingrain these smells of luxury into your mind.

Now taste the money. What does the money taste like, and what are the tastes you can afford with your money? Is it a luxury car, is it a new home, is it expensive trips? Whatever it is, know that if you can dream it, you can manifest it. Visualize now all those things you can make possible in your life.

As you lie back in the field, allow your senses to open up and feel the things that are possible in your life. Dream big. Notice how wonderful and soft the money is to lie in. It is almost as though it sticks to you and you cannot get it off. It is as though you have become a money magnet. It is as if the money has always been there for you, but you could not see it. The heavens were waiting for you just to ask for it in a clear and precise way.

As you are sitting in the field of money, the money seems to be taking on a mind of its own and begins speaking to you. There is an internal knowing that the abundance of the Earth is available to you any time you wish to ask for it. You suddenly begin to feel a different vibrational energy in your body. Notice that energy; notice how that vibration feels. It may be a little in a tingle in your hand, or you may feel it a lot as a whole body shiver. No matter how you feel it, know now that you are resonating a different vibrational frequency from any you have ever thought possible.

That energy that you have now manifested can actually attract wealth, health, and happiness. Make the decision now to take this vibrational energy back with you to the consciousness. Notice that words like "I can," "I will," and "I Am" are now a part of your vocabulary.

As you think these words, notice the effect they have upon your vibrational level. Notice the power in these words, and make the decision now never to allow anyone, ever again, to tell you what you can and cannot do.

You ARE capable of making your own decisions, making your own happiness, making your own living, and collecting money in ways you always thought possible.

Take a few minutes and reflect on your newfound courage and personal energy. You know now that any time you need this energy, you may sit down, take a few breaths, and bring forward this energy just by thinking, "I can do this—all is possible."

If that is okay with you, continue breathing normally and notice the incredible grounding and power coming from the root, spleen, and solar plexus chakra. Know now that you WILL move forward, like a powerhouse, saying, "I can and I will." Plant your feet, and say it out loud: "I can and I will." Say it again and again, believing it stronger with each passing moment. Know that you know something now that you always have known, but to know it now makes you more powerful than you ever thought possible. It is your secret, and you can choose to share it with the world, if that is what you choose to do. With that in mind, take a deep breath and open your eyes only when you are ready. After you open your eyes, continue breathing normally and take a minute for the body to stabilize. Get yourself a big drink of water because you have just expended a lot of energy. Then get a pad of paper and write down your experiences. If you don't write them down, you will forget them. Peace be with you.

Intention Boxes or Wealth Jar

An intention box or wealth jar is a place where we put physical objects with mental intentions of something happening. The intention box should be filled to the brim with those things you wish to manifest. I recommend items of wealth, health, and happiness. You can make your box unique to you, or you can use traditional wealth bowls.

Listed below are some ideas for your intention box. They have brought good results to me.

A wealth box should be made of wood or nice cardboard with a lid to hold the energy in place. A mirror in the lid of the box will enhance and magnify the contents of the box. Use the type of box that resonates with your energy. If you wish to use a glass wealth jar, it should be narrow at the top or have a lid to keep the money in.

First and foremost, place a picture of your family or friends in your box. On the back of the photo, write a message signifying long life, happiness, and wealth. This keeps you connected to family and them to you.

Include nine I Ching coins tied together with a red ribbon. Place them in a red envelope for wealth. Include a large denomination bill in another red envelope. The more real money in the box, the better.

Include eight different types of semiprecious stones, especially jade and amethyst. Read the sector on chakras, and use the stones helpful in achieving your life aspirations. Include any crystal, especially quartz. It increases the chi in your wealth bowl. Include pearls or luminescent beads that glow with inner life. Use Kyanite or tourmaline to disperse negative energy in your box.

Include pictures of sailing ships or a miniature ship to symbolize your ship coming in. Some red envelopes have the “golden” ships already on them.

Include a never-ending knot for longevity in business.

Include an eight-sided object for balance, such as an eight-sided ba gua mirror.

Include anything that symbolizes wealth, happiness, and health you would like to manifest. Ideas may include healthy food and happy Buddhas.

For a prosperous business venture, include soil from an already prosperous business. Place the soil in a red envelope. Ask for permission, or replace the spoonful of dirt with some from your home.

In the box, place pictures of yourself at a healthiest time in your life. Use your imagination. If you wish to travel, include travel brochures.

Make sure to have something in the bowl that symbolizes the five elements: water (ship), wood (paper money), fire (red envelope), earth (stones), and metal (coins).

Do the three secret reinforcements, creating your intention and always saying the phrase "with harm to none." Every day, reinforce the energy of your bowl with your mental energy. Remember, to ridicule the ritual is an insult to the mysterious energy that governs the feng shui adjustments. Insults will minimize the effect of the mysterious energy of feng shui.

Remember: this is a red envelope cure. Please put a donation in a red envelope, and mail it to your favorite charity in the name of mankind. This generosity will be returned tenfold.

Other Modalities of Energy Work to Enhance Your Life and Improve Lifestyle

Traditional Chinese Medicine: TCM looks at all aspects of the human body and environment. The doctor, then, may use herbs, acupuncture, and feng shui to help improve health.

Acupuncture and Acupressure: This is the practice of applying needles or pressure to the different energy points or meridian points of the body. This pressure either stimulates or slows down the energy going through these points, thus promoting better health.

Massage: Massage is a method of relieving stress in the muscles and tissues of the body and allowing toxins to leave the system. There are numerous methods of massage, so it is important to apply the appropriate method to your body. Ask questions when choosing a massage therapist. Keep searching until you receive the answers that you feel are right for you.

Reiki: Reiki is a form of channeling energy into the body by a series of handholds over the body. Reiki has its origins in the Asian system but has developed quickly in the West.

Flower Essences and Essential Oils: These items use the vibratory frequency of plants to help remove and resolve emotional blocks. They have been used successfully since biblical times.

Energy Cultivations: These include yoga, tai chi, qigong, and meditation. All of these exercises promote vital energy into the body while restoring harmony to the mind.

Hypnotherapy and Neuro-Linguistic Programming: Both of these are valuable in helping release emotional blocks and replacing them with a positive outlook.

Always ask for credentials and certifications of practitioners with whom you are working.

Conclusion

If you follow the instructions in this book, you should begin see changes in your life immediately.

Start with the feng shui of your body. Do the chakra grounding exercises and some of the meditations to help define your goals clearly. Use this technique to help remove blocks holding you back from your dreams and goals. What is holding you back? What are your fears and doubts? What are your assets? Write these down.

Become aware of what your environment is saying to you. Is it supporting your dreams and visions? If not, change it. De-clutter and remodel with color and objects of goal setting, or have a garage sale and start completely over. Go through your home closely: look at every object in every nook and cranny. Make sure everything is exactly what you want in your life. Always be aware of the ever-changing Earth energy and ever-changing energy of man. What you may have wanted yesterday may not be what you want today. It is okay to change your mind. Change means growth.

The answers to the following questions will help you to get clear on what you want and what is blocking your energy.

What are some objects that bring me pleasure and why?

What are some objects that bring me distress and why?

Are friends and family encouraging me to be a better person and accomplish my goals? Name those people who you can turn to for support, those who believe in you.

Name other sources or places you can turn for support, such as women's groups, prayer circles, churches, and organizations.

Exercise daily. This keeps the mind sharp and expansive.

Do mind or mental activity, such as the optical illusion exercises, crossword puzzles, word games, mathematical calculations, or psychic games with yourself. Look at the clouds for pictures; try to see auras around objects and people. Look for things that are not visible to the first glance. Read, study, and research your own information.

Keep your senses sharp. Pay stricter attention to how things smell, taste, appear, feel, or sound. Go beyond seeing with the eyes and hearing with the ears. Hear what is not being said; see what is not being shown. Allow taste to come in through smell. Most of all, allow the body to feel the air, feel the environment, and feel the emotions. Sense the energy in the room. Pay attention to the little voices in your head. Trust your intuition.

Learn to tell the difference between a guess and a feeling of surety. Keep practicing until you get it right. You may not always be right, but I venture you will get much better at it.

Find commitment and tenacity to carry out your dreams and goals, no matter what happens or who makes comments about it. Most importantly, meditate and keep your mind clear and your goals prioritized. Fight for your right to be.

I hope this gets you started on your journey, the feng shui way to self-awareness, and the manifestation of your highest potential. I wish you peace and harmony in your journey. Remember, this is only a small tip of the iceberg. Each day, seek out new teachers, and keep your mind open to the unknown.

I would like to end with some Charles Schultz philosophy, the creator of the Peanuts comic strip. He asked for all of us to think about facts similar to these:

Can you name the ten wealthiest people in the world or the last three winners of Miss America? Do you know who won the last Academy Award movie or NBA finals?

How did you do, and do you really care?

The point is, none of you remember these types of facts from yesterday unless they directly involve your life. There will always be famous people with great accomplishments, but after the headlines fade, does it really matter?

Your life or accomplishments may not be headliners, but the events that involve you and your circle of influence are important to someone. Just because someone famous has learned to market himself or herself a little better than you have does not make their accomplishments any more important than yours. We are all where we are for a reason. This reason is to make a difference.

Think about these questions and see how they affect your thoughts and memories.

List a few people who have helped inspire you to overcome adversity. These are friends who cried with you, felt your pain, and still stayed by your side. They encouraged you to keep on. They kept your glass half full when it felt half empty. Call them and thank them.

Name a person or persons who encouraged or helped you achieve something worthwhile. These are your cheerleaders, people who believe in you, people who keep cheering you on no matter how impossible the situation may look. They keep you on track. Call them and thank them.

Name a person or persons who have made you feel appreciated and special. These people love the little things about you. They love the way you look in the morning when you wake up. They love the way you look when your face is sunburned and your hair is windblown. They don't love you for how much money you make or what you can do for them. They love you for you. They may not even realize what your accomplishments are or what it is you do when you are not with them. They just love you. Call them and thank them.

Think of three or more people with whom you wish spend time or enjoy spending time. If you were stranded in the middle of nowhere for a very long time, with whom do you want to be? These people are the most important people in your life. Honor them and let them know how you feel. Spend quality time with them. Life is short. Call them and tell them.

Now you think of someone who encouraged you to move on when you were feeling down. Think of all of these people in reverse, people to whom you were the cheerleader. Think of the people who you love unconditionally no matter what.

The people who make a difference in your life are not the ones with the most credentials, the most money, or the most awards. They are the ones who touch your life every day. They are the ones you personally interact with and care for. As you are manifesting your highest potential, make sure not to forget what is really important, and be of service to yourself and humankind first and foremost.

Keep in touch. E-mail me with your stories of success, change, or challenge.

designwisdom@yahoo.com.

> Because for now, for you,
> The sidewalk ends and the road begins . . .
>
> —George Strait, *Pure Country*
>
> Love, Mary

About the Author

Mary Dillin-Shurtleff, FSID, CHT

Motivational Speaker, Six-Sensory Practitioner

Mary Dillin-Shurtleff of Design Wisdom is an author, national and international motivational speaker, clinical hypnotherapist, feng shui interior designer, theta healer, and six-sensory practitioner.

Mary has taken energy healing into the twenty-first century, using behavior modification methods and feng shui in tandem to change the pattern of behavior within the home to facilitate change within body—thus bringing the home and body into alignment with each other.

Mary has been in the metaphysical field since 1989. She certified in 1991 as a clinical hypnotherapist under the tutelage of Virgil Hayes and Betty Finnas of the Hypnotism Training Center in Salt Lake City, Utah. Mary studied with and admires the work of the late Ormand McGill and his work with the mystic. Mary is a member of the American Council of Hypnotist Examiners as well as the National Guild of Hypnotists, Inc. She has been featured as a speaker at the National Hypnosis Conventions on the topic of how your environment can affect your behavior. Mary is also a certified six-sensory practitioner under the umbrella of Sonia Choquette, world-renowned spiritual teacher and psychic of Chicago, Illinois.

Mary certified in Form School, Eight Mansions, and Flying Stars with Master Peter Leung. She is also certified in the Black Hat School of Feng Shui. She underwent advanced geomancy training—the detection of electromagnetic energy and geopathic stresses—with Dominique Susani of Spain, and Mary attended the China Studies Program in China with Helen and James Jay. Other teachers with whom she has had the opportunity to study are Lillian Too, Tao Tan, and Michael Scott Kelley. Mary is a Gold School member of the International Feng Shui guild, and she trains practitioners /coaches in the basics of feng shui interior design and the intuitive arts, in compliance with the standards of the IFSG.

Mary has studied theta healing and has earned certifications in the basics of theta healing, advanced theta healing, and intuitive anatomy under the tutelage of Melinda Lee of Orem, Utah.

Mary developed and instructed a credit and noncredit class on the basics of feng shui at the University of Utah in Salt Lake City, Utah. This class incorporated feng shui and behavior modification methods to facilitate stress management. Mary has been instrumental in bringing feng shui into the mainstream intellectual field in Utah.

Mary has been a featured speaker nationwide and is a regular feature author for the *Changing Times Magazine*, available online at www.changingtimesmagazine.com. You can also hear Mary on "Journey into the Light," on www.blogtalkradio.com/journeyintothelight. Mary has been featured on the "World's Greatest! . . ." program, which appears on the Ion Channel. Mary has a YouTube link at www.youtube.com/watch?v=0m3Wm-V7yu0.

Mary Shurtleff is the author of the book Reconnecting the Spirit: Seeing the Possibilities as well as the books *The Alchemy of Quantum Mind Feng Shui* and *A Reference Guide for the Students of Feng Shui*, available in most bookstores. She has recorded two audio hypnosis CDs entitled *Quantum Mind Feng Shui: Opening the Third Eye of Consciousness—Projecting Dreams into Reality* and *If You Can Dream It, You Can Be It*, a weight management/self-esteem tool designed to help you transform your mental and physical image of self.

Mary believes that diversity in educational studies is important to keep your mind sharp and your wisdom heightened. When these modalities are properly applied, Mary believes it is as close to magic as one can get.

Mary owns and operates Design Wisdom–Feng Shui in Salt Lake City, where she does private consulting, speaking engagements, and seminars. See Mary at www.maryshurtleff.com or see the updated feng shui monthly aspect blogs at www.maryshurtleff.blogspot.com.

References

(Arranged in order of importance of material used.)

Shurtleff, Mary. *A Reference Guide for Students of Feng Shui*. Horizon Publishing: Bountiful, Utah, 2000.

Reichstein, Gail. *Wood Becomes Water: Chinese Medicine in Everyday Life*. Kodansha International, 1998.

Shinn, Florence Scovel. *The Wisdom of Florence Scovel Shinn*. Fireside Books: New York, 1989.

Hay, Louise. *Heal Your Body*. Hay House: Carlsbad, California, 1982.

Linn, Denise. *The Secret Language of Signs*. Ballantine Books: New York, 1996.

Essential Oil Desk Reference, Compiled by Essential Science Publishing: Orem, Utah, May 2000.

Andrews, Ted. *Animal Speak*. Llewellyn Publications: St. Paul, Minnesota, 2003.

Yamamoto, Tsunetomo. *Bushido: The Way of the Samurai*. Justin F. Stone, ed. Square One Publishers: Garden City Park, New York, 2001.

Choquette, Sonia. *Trust Your Vibes*. Hay House: Carlsbad, California, 2005.

Christensen, Debra. Personal Research on Chakras, Ba Gua, and Essential Oils. Salt Lake City, Utah, 1998.

Finnas, Betty. Personal Research on Chakras and Meditations. Sandy, Utah, 1995.

Tan, Tao. Training Notes. Salt Lake City, Utah, 1999.

Lillian Too, Training Notes, Los Angeles, California, 2002.

Susani, Dominique. Training Notes. 2002.

Jay, James, and Helen Jay. Training Manual, Nevada City, California, 2000.

Stasney, Sharon. Training Manual, Salt Lake City, Utah. 1998.

Bridges, Lillian Garnier. Workshop Notes and www.lotusinstitute.com/5ElementsOfFood.html, 2002.

McGill, Ormand. Violet Flame, Workshop Notes and Audio Cassette, 1992.

References

Breenan, Barbara Ann. *Hands of Light*. Bantam Books: New York, 1987.

Mesko, Sabrina. *Healing Mudras: Yoga for Your Hands*. Ballantine Publishing Company: New York, 2000.

Mella, Dorothee L. *Stone Power*. Warner Books, Inc.: New York, 1988.

Melody. *Love Is in the Earth*. Earth Love Publishing House: Wheat Ridge, Colorado, 1995.

The Words and Inspirations of Mother Teresa. Love. Blue Mountain Arts, Inc.: Boulder, Colorado, 2007.

The Encyclopedia Americana, American Corporation, 1962.

Salter, Donna. *Finding Your Wings*. Workshop Manual. Salt Lake City, Utah, 1992.

Patton, Donna, and Jeannie Patton. *Expanding Your Wings*. Workshop Manual. Salt Lake City, Utah, 1992.

Kelley, Michael Scott. Four-Pillar Seminar. Austin, Texas, 2000.

Martin, Ed. *Meditation of Cellular Release.* Work. ACHE Convention, Austin, Texas, 1995.

Too, Lillian. *The Complete Illustrated Guide to Feng Shui*. Element Books Ltd.: Dorset, UK, 1996.

Rivera A, Adalberto. *Mysteries of Chichen Itza*. San Fernando: Mexico, 2001.

Barber, Susan, with Drunvalo and Ken Page. 2004. "Entity Clearing." www.spiritofmaat.com/archive/aug4/clearing.htm.

Too, Lillian. 2009. www.wofs.com.

Rodier, Hugo. Interview by Author. Comprehensive Pioneer Medical Center. 1999.

Reconnecting Your Spirit reaches beyond the basic principles of feng shui to explore a combination of information on man's spiritual connection to God, theta/gamma healing, development of the six-sensory connection, hypnosis/behavior modification methods, power of thoughts, impact of words, metaphors and signs, and feng shui.

Reconnecting Your Spirit is designed to help those who wish to decode their childhood programming, generational tendencies, and word formations to discover who they truly are and what they desire.

A New Normal: The Connected Being, the third book in this series, takes you further into the realms of spirit and intuitions and is scheduled for release in 2011.

Available through www.MaryShurtleff.com

CPSIA information can be obtained
at www.ICGtesting.com
Printed in the USA
LVHW061150100223
739195LV00009B/233

9 780983 089216